LOVE to READ!

ACTIVITIES TO FOSTER A LOVE OF READING

BY CINDY BARDEN

ILLUSTRATIONS BY CORBIN HILLAM

Teaching & Learning Company

1204 Buchanan St., P.O. Box 10
Carthage, IL 62321

This book belongs to

_____

This book was developed for the Teaching & Learning Company by The Good Neighbor Press, Inc., Grand Junction, CO.

Cover illustration by Corbin Hillam

Copyright © 1995, Teaching & Learning Company

ISBN No. 1-57310-032-3

Printing No. 987654321

Teaching & Learning Company
1204 Buchanan St., P.O. Box 10
Carthage, IL 62321

TABLE OF CONTENTS

Dear Teacher,

> "He that loves reading, has everything within his reach."
> *William Godwin*

Do you love to read? I do. We share our enthusiasm with our students when we show them we are excited about reading. You can do this by telling your students about books or stories you've read. You can read aloud to your class every day, even if it's only for 5 or 10 minutes. Read poems you loved at their age. Read short stories. Read novels, a chapter at a time. Provide free reading time in class. To get students started on an assigned novel, read the first chapter or two out loud. Help students get the reading habit, so they too will "love to read."

Invite students to write book reviews and recommendations on 3" x 5" (7.62 x 12.7 cm) index cards. Keep the cards in a file box, alphabetically by title. When other students are looking for something to read, they can check the file for suggestions.

Listen to recommendations for good books made by students. If they've found a book they are enthusiastic about and one you haven't read, read it.

The first section of *Love to Read!* includes activities that can be used with a wide variety of literature and suggestions for several different types of book reports. Some activities are designed to help students increase their vocabulary, a skill so important to becoming good readers.

You will also find activities specific to a variety of stories, books and poems from easy reading, like *The Lorax* and "There Was an Old Man with a Beard" to more difficult reading for advanced students, like *A Wrinkle in Time* and "The Bells." When not copyrighted, the poems are included in the activities. The other poems and stories used are well-known and can easily be found in many anthologies for class use.

The appendix includes bulletin board ideas for encouraging students to read, reader award certificates, a list of suggested poetry reading, a list of Newbery Medal Award books and an answer key.

The ability to read well, an enjoyment and understanding of many types of literature and the desire to learn more through reading are invaluable gifts we give to our students. I hope your students enjoy the activities and "love to read" as much as I do.

Sincerely,

Cindy

Cindy Barden

█▚ LOVE TO READ

Design a poster for the theme "LOVE TO READ." You may use words, drawings, magazine pictures and/or designs.

WEEKLY READING LOG

Get into the reading habit by spending some time every day with a book, magazine or newspaper. To keep track of what you read, fill in the information below every day. Turn in your weekly log to your teacher.

Monday, Date: _____
Book title: _____
Author: _____
Number of pages read: _____
Name of newspaper or magazine:
_____
Titles of articles: _____
_____
Other reading: _____
Time spent reading: _____

Tuesday, Date: _____
Book title: _____
Author: _____
Number of pages read: _____
Name of newspaper or magazine:
_____
Titles of articles: _____
_____
Other reading: _____
Time spent reading: _____

Wednesday, Date: _____
Book title: _____
Author: _____
Number of pages read: _____
Name of newspaper or magazine:
_____
Titles of articles: _____
_____
Other reading: _____
Time spent reading: _____

Thursday, Date: _____
Book title: _____
Author: _____
Number of pages read: _____
Name of newspaper or magazine:
_____
Titles of articles: _____
_____
Other reading: _____
Time spent reading: _____

Friday, Date: _____
Book title: _____
Author: _____
Number of pages read: _____
Name of newspaper or magazine:
_____
Titles of articles: _____
_____
Other reading: _____
Time spent reading: _____

Saturday, Date: _____
Book title: _____
Author: _____
Number of pages read: _____
Name of newspaper or magazine:
_____
Titles of articles: _____
_____
Other reading: _____
Time spent reading: _____

Sunday, Date: _____
Book title: _____
Author: _____
Number of pages read: _____
Name of newspaper or magazine:
_____
Titles of articles: _____
_____
Other reading: _____
Time spent reading: _____

I verify this log is correct: _____

BOOK REPORTS WITH A TWIST

Tired of doing the same old type of book report over and over? How about something different? Instead of writing about the author, main characters and summarizing the plot, give a demonstration report.

For your demonstration report, you can use any of the ideas listed, or your own ideas, whatever works best for you. The only requirement is to have fun preparing and giving your report.

- Design a chart or graph and explain it to the class.

- Design a poster about the book.

- Draw a four-panel cartoon for the book.

- Design a book jacket for the book.

- Demonstrate something you learned in the book.

- Prepare a menu based on the book and characters.

- Make up and sing a theme song for the book.

- Do a dance the main character might have done.

- Give a puppet show based on the book.

- Write a two-minute radio commercial for the book.

- Explain how the book could be an Olympic event.

- Design a place mat about your book.

- Make up a word game or puzzle.

- Draw a map of the places in the book.

- Explain how this book could be a video game.

- Write a poem based on the book.

- Make a tape recording or video of dialogue between you and the main character.

- Dress like the main character. Explain what you're wearing and why.

- If this book were made into a movie, what actors and actresses would you choose to play the parts? Why?

▉ HOW TO . . .

"**H**ow to" books are available for almost anything you might want to learn, make or do. You can learn a new skill, game or sport or improve your skills with a "how to" book. You can learn how to start a new hobby, solve a problem, build or repair something. Would you like to design a Japanese garden? Prune a tree? Build a sand castle? Use a new software program? Repair a bicycle? Explore the information highway? Do a magic trick? Save money? Earn money? Raise earthworms?

Select a "how to" book on any subject that interests you. After you read the book, complete the information below.

Book title: _____

Author: _____

This book teaches people how to _____

_____

_____

Why did you select this topic? _____

_____

_____

How can you use the information in this book?_____

_____

_____

_____

What is the best piece of advice you learned from reading this book? _____

_____

Were the directions clear? Explain your answer. _____

_____

_____

How could this book have been better?_____

_____

_____

Give a class demonstration of one thing you learned from this book.

GET TO KNOW SOMEONE

A true story written by a person about his or her life is called an **autobiography**. If someone else writes about a person's life, it's called a **biography**.

Select a biography or autobiography about someone you'd like to learn more about. You could choose a book about a famous leader, a baseball player, an artist, an astronaut or anyone at all. After reading the book, fill in the blanks below.

Person the book is about: _____

Book title: _____

Author: _____

Why did you choose this person to read about? _____

_____

When did this person live? From _____ to _____

Where did this person live? _____

What is this person best known for? _____

List three interesting facts you learned about this person.

    1. _____

    2. _____

    3. _____

What was the most difficult thing this person ever had to do? _____

What was the person's greatest accomplishment? _____

What did you like best about this person? _____

What did you like least about this person? _____

Who do you know that reminds you of this person? How are they alike? How are they different?

_____

_____

Would you like to meet this person? Why or why not?

_____

_____

Why should other people read this book?

_____

_____

BEGINNINGS, MIDDLES AND ENDS

To be complete, a story must have a beginning, a middle and an ending. Refer to a book or story you've read recently to answer the questions below.

Title: _____

♥ ♥ ♥ ♥ ♥ ♥ ♥

The **beginning** of a story introduces the main character and his or her problem. A good beginning gets readers interested in reading the rest of the story.

Describe the main characters at the beginning of the story. _____

_____

What problem does the main character have? _____

_____

Does this story have a good beginning? Why or why not? _____

_____

♥ ♥ ♥ ♥ ♥ ♥ ♥

The **middle** of a story tells what the character does and what happens.

What does the character do? _____

_____

What happens as a result of the character's actions? _____

_____

♥ ♥ ♥ ♥ ♥ ♥ ♥

The **ending** of a story tells how the characters solve the problem and how the story ends. A good ending answers most of the questions you had while reading the story. Good endings can be sad or happy.

How did the character solve the problem? _____

_____

How does the story end? _____

_____

Did this story have a good ending? Why or why not?_____

_____

If you didn't like the ending, how do you think it should have ended? _____

_____

▐▌ WORD POWER

The more words students know and understand, the better readers they become. Help your students increase their reading vocabulary with these suggestions:

Match the Definitions: Write the definitions of words on index cards, one per card. Make enough cards so each student will have three or four. Write a word on the chalkboard. Ask the class, "Who has the definition for this word?" The student with the correct definition reads it to the class and uses the word in a sentence.

If no one gives the correct definition, ask for a volunteer to define the word.   Then the student with the correct definition can respond and read the definition. Ask for volunteers to use the word in a sentence. Cards can be redistributed and used several times.

Word Power: Use the page entitled "It Pays to Enrich Your Word Power" from the *Reader's Digest* to add new words to your students' vocabulary.

Discussion Topics
Why should we learn new words?
What is "word power"?
How do words give us power?

Word Cards: Write one word per card on index cards, enough so each student will have three or four. Ask students to look up the word in the dictionary and write a short definition on the card; then write a sentence using the word.

Students can trade cards with classmates every day. Challenge students to use their new words at least twice a day.

Other Vocabulary Activities: Vocabulary activities can be used in any order or in conjunction with other activities in this book. The following pages include additional activities to increase students' reading vocabulary: Vocabulary Scavenger Hunt; Compound Capers; Adopt-a-Word; In the Beginning; At the End; The Same, but Different; The Same and Not the Same and Vocabulary Bingo.

Vocabulary Bingo: Use 24 index cards. Write one word and a short definition on each card. After you read each word and definition to the class, ask students to write the word on any square of their Bingo Words card. Continue until all 24 squares are filled.

To play, select any word card at random and read the definition. Students can use buttons, small squares of paper or other small items to cover the square of the word that matches the definition you read.

VOCABULARY SCAVENGER HUNT

In some scavenger hunts people search for unusual items. This is a vocabulary scavenger hunt. The only place you'll need to look is in the nearest dictionary. Work with a partner to find all the words from A to Z needed to complete the scavenger hunt. Write the correct word from the box in the blank after the definition.

ambiguous	gregarious	loquacious	quiescence	verification
bilingual	holocaust	minuscule	rigorous	wainwright
coalition	inept	nuance	sequential	xanthic
deciduous	jocose	ominous	trepidation	yowl
egalitarian	kinetic	pompous	unilateral	zenith
feign				

1. Slight degree of difference in meaning _____

2. A temporary alliance _____

3. Very small _____

4. To pretend _____

5. Fear _____

6. Joking _____

7. Inactive or dormant _____

8. In order _____

9. One who makes or repairs wagons _____

10. Related to motion _____

11. Harsh _____

12. A long, loud, sad cry _____

13. Able to speak two languages well _____

14. Full of self-importance _____

15. Belief that everyone has equal rights _____

16. Talkative _____

17. Yellow _____

18. Large scale destruction of life _____

19. One-sided _____

20. Having more than one meaning _____

21. The highest point _____

22. Threatening _____

23. Not competent _____

24. Trees that shed their leaves each year _____

25. Proof _____

26. Fond of being among people _____

◰ VOCABULARY BINGO

Your teacher will read a list of 24 words and their definitions. Write the words in any square below, in any order. Write only one word in each square. To play, cover the correct word on your Bingo Words card when your teacher reads the definition for that word.

W	O	R	D	S
		FREE		

◼ COMPOUND CAPERS

Words that are formed by joining two short words to make a longer word are called **compound words**. Add a word between the two words in each row to form two compound words. The blanks show the number of letters needed. Work with a partner to fill in the missing words. Using a dictionary may be helpful.

Here's an example. If the words were LIGHT ___ ___ ___ ___ ___ FLY, the middle word would be HOUSE (*lighthouse* and *housefly*).

1.	BREAK	___ ___ ___ ___	FALL
2.	BAND	___ ___ ___ ___ ___	BY
3.	STAR	___ ___ ___ ___	TAIL
4.	LIGHT	___ ___ ___ ___ ___	BOAT
5.	OUT	___ ___ ___ ___	YARD
6.	UP	___ ___ ___ ___	TOP
7.	BELL	___ ___ ___ ___	SCOTCH
8.	PASS	___ ___ ___	STONE
9.	TEA	___ ___ ___ ___	BOARD
10.	WALK	___ ___ ___ ___	SIDE
11.	PAPER	___ ___ ___ ___	HORSE
12.	WATER	___ ___ ___	POST
13.	MARK	___ ___ ___ ___	CAST
14.	HORSE	___ ___ ___ ___	GROUND
15.	OFF	___ ___ ___ ___	BALL
16.	BAR	___ ___ ___ ___	HOP
17.	BED	___ ___ ___ ___	MARK
18.	PLAY	___ ___ ___ ___ ___ ___	WATER
19.	SIDE	___ ___ ___ ___	PAPER
20.	FISH	___ ___ ___ ___	LIGHT
21.	CAST	___ ___ ___	HAND
22.	HAND	___ ___ ___	PARK

Select two of the compound words you made above. Write them below with a short definition.

Word	**Definition**
_____	_____
	_____
_____	_____
	_____

▌▌ADOPT-A-WORD

Select one of the words from the list in the box or from a list your teacher provides. You can adopt that word and give it a good home. You will need to make others familiar with your new word so they can call it by name.

ambulatory	regicide	therapeutic	manipulate
nemesis	convoluted	regimental	nefarious
additive	capitol	peculiar	triage
generalize	benevolent	adversary	monopoly
Renaissance	apartheid	condensation	aqueduct
coniferous	desalinization	evaporation	magma
herbicide	hydroelectric	literacy	autonomy
archipelago	substantiate	temporal	kinetic
utilization	harmonic	schematic	delicacy
consequence	memorandum	efficacious	instrumental
satellite	undermine	circumference	intersect
conjoin	reciprocal	hemisphere	computation
abolition	amnesty	autocracy	confederation

Your adopted word: _____

Meaning of your word:_____

_____

What part(s) of speech is your new word? _____

Two antonyms (words that mean the opposite) for your word:

_____

Two synonyms (words that mean the same) for your word:

_____

Use your new word in a sentence. _____

_____

Write a bumper sticker for your new word.

_____

Why is this word special to you? _____

_____

Do a class demonstration of your word. You may use one of the ideas below or one of your own.

■ Pantomime the word.
■ Do an illustration for the word.
■ Make up a song or jingle for the word.
■ Make up an ad to promote your word.
■ Give the history of the word.

IN THE BEGINNING

A prefix comes at the beginning of a word. You can often figure out the meaning of a new word if you know what the prefix means.

Study these prefixes and their meanings:

Prefix	Meaning	Prefix	Meaning
Ante-	Before	Anti- or Ant-	Against
Bi-	Two	Co- or Con-	Together
Im-, In-, Il-	Not	Inter-	Between
Intra-	Within	Mal-	Bad
Mis-	Wrong	Non-	Not
Post-	After	Pre-	Before
Pro-	For	Re-	Again
Retro-	Backward	Semi-	Half
Sub-	Under	Trans-	Across
Tri-	Three	Un-	Not

Define the words below using the meanings you learned. Write your definitions without using a dictionary.

transatlantic _____

recharge _____

antedate _____

nonviolent _____

unstable _____

pregame _____

postgame _____

Underline the prefixes in these words:

semiconscious	submarine	transcontinental	illegible
cooperate	conserve	misdeed	malcontent
pretest	postscript	tricycle	bicentennial
retroactive	interactive	inactive	intrastate

Select three of the prefixes listed above. For each prefix, write two words that begin with that prefix.

Prefix   **Words**

1. _____   _____   _____

2. _____   _____   _____

3. _____   _____   _____

TLC10032 Copyright © Teaching & Learning Company, Carthage, IL 62321

◼▦ AT THE END

A suffix comes at the end of a word. You can often figure out the meaning of a new word if you know what the suffix means.

Study these suffixes and their meanings.

Suffix	Meaning	Suffix	Meaning
-able or -ible	Capable of being	-less	Without
-dom	State of being	-ness	State of being
-ful	Filled with	-y	Filled with
-er or -or	One who does something		

Define the words below using the meanings you learned. Write your definitions without using a dictionary.

juicy _____

snowy _____

sadness _____

happiness _____

lovable _____

freedom _____

actor _____

baker _____

friendless _____

careless _____

harmful _____

Underline the suffixes in these words:

sloppy	adjustable	filthy	ceaseless	consumer
inspector	hopeless	colorful	illness	gentleness
kingdom	cheerful	giver	auditor	moveable

Select three of the suffixes listed above. For each suffix, write two words that begin with that suffix.

	Suffix	Words
1.	_____	_____ _____
2.	_____	_____ _____
3.	_____	_____ _____

THE SAME, BUT DIFFERENT

Homonyms are words that are pronounced the same, but spelled differently, like *too, two* and *to*. Homonyms have different meanings, so it's important to use the right one.

Write a homonym for each word listed below.

bear _____   hair _____

pane _____   sew _____

tow _____   cents _____

sale _____   mail _____

tale _____   ferry _____

four _____   plane _____

eye _____   reign _____

main _____   hoe _____

blew _____   knew _____

flew _____   pale _____

Circle the correct homonym to complete each sentence.

1. The (bear, bare) was very (hairy, harry).

2. Jon bought (two, to, too) (sails, sales) for his (sail, sale) boat.

3. People who (so, sew) can save money on (clothes, close).

4. (Four, For) plus (two, too, to) equals six.

5. My friends are going (two, too, to) London. (They're, Their, There) going to visit (they're, their, there) relatives when they get (they're, their, there).

6. Why are (some, sum) words pronounced the same, but spelled differently? It doesn't make (cents, sense, scents).

7. Rita (won, one) the spelling (bee, be).

8. If you had (two, to, too) (pears, pairs) for lunch, would (you, ewe) have eaten (a pair of pears) or (a pear of pairs)?

9. Jake (gnu, knew, new) he wanted a (gnu, new, knew) (blue, blew) (pair, pear) of shoes.

10. Sometimes it can be a (pane, pain) to remember (which, witch) word is the (right, write) (won, one).

Work with a partner to make a list of homonyms. Can you find at least 25 pairs besides the ones listed above?

THE SAME AND NOT THE SAME

Words that have the same or similar meanings, like *big* and *large*, are called **synonyms**.

On another sheet of paper, write synonyms for the words in the list below. Use a dictionary if you need it. Remember, use only one word, not an entire definition.

like	talented	future	eternal
once	happy	descend	child
frown	leave	get	item
past	slow	opposite	similar
worry	responsible	honest	capable

Make a list of five more words and their synonyms.

1. _____   _____

2. _____   _____

3. _____   _____

4. _____   _____

5. _____   _____

Words that mean the opposite, like *big* and *little*, are called **antonyms**.

On another sheet of paper, write antonyms for the words in the list below. Most dictionaries list antonyms if you need help.

late	slow
tall	thin
future	remember
hurry	stop
open	high
absent	smile
neat	parent
ceiling	ascend
listen	hairy
kind	happy

Make a list of five more words and their antonyms.

1. _____   _____

2. _____   _____

3. _____   _____

4. _____   _____

5. _____   _____

▮⬛ WHY READ?

Why do people read books? Why do you read? Fill in the lines around the sun with reasons why people read.

One caption for this page could be: "Books Brighten Your Life." Write another caption for this page.

_____

▇ FAMOUS PHRASES

Here's a different way to report on a book you've read.

Title: _____

Author: _____

Read these famous phrases. Select one that applies to the book you've read and explain how it applies. Put an *X* by the phrase you chose.

_____ A penny saved, is a penny earned.

_____ Where there's a will, there's a way.

_____ If you lie down with dogs, you get up with fleas.

_____ Money is the root of all evil.

_____ A stitch in time saves nine.

_____ People who live in glass houses shouldn't throw stones.

_____ A rolling stone gathers no moss.

_____ Every cloud has a silver lining.

_____ Look before you leap.

_____ Honesty is the best policy.

_____ The early bird catches the worm.

_____ Practice what you preach.

_____ Haste makes waste.

_____ All that glitters is not gold.

_____ Opportunity knocks but once.

_____ You can't judge a book by its cover.

_____ Beauty is only skin deep.

_____ The grass is always greener on the other side of the fence.

_____ One rotten apple spoils the bushel.

_____

_____

_____

_____

_____

_____

_____

_____

_____

▐░ TIME LINE

A time line shows important events that occurred during a given period. A time line could be drawn for a single day, with the hours marked off, or for a longer period of time. A historical time line could cover hundreds of years.

Here's an example of a historical time line:

Your time line:

Make a time line starting the year you were born. Write at least one important event that occurred each year since then. Use the back of this page for your time line. Turn the paper the long way so you have more room. Your time line can take more than one line if you need the room to write.

A story time line:

Select a book or story you've read. During what time period does the action take place?

From _____ to _____

Think about the major events of the story. Make a time line for this story. List important events that occurred and when they happened. Use more than one line if you need the room to write.

▍▓ ALL ABOUT _____

As you read a story, you get to know the characters. You learn how they look, what they like and dislike. You learn how they feel about some things.

Some authors give more detailed information about characters than others. To complete this activity, you may use what the author tells you about a character as well as your own imagination.

Book or story title: _____

Author: _____

Character: _____

Wherever possible, use the information from the story to complete the information. When the information can't be found in the story, fill in the information with what you think would be correct. Put an * by the information you didn't find in the book.

Age: _____   Height: _____   Weight: _____   Eye color: _____

Hair color: _____   Skin color: _____

Type of clothing usually worn: _____

When and where does the character live? _____

Describe the character's house. _____

_____

Who is the character's best friend? _____

List the character's favorites.

Food: _____   Song: _____

Color: _____   Sport: _____

Hobby: _____   Place to be alone: _____

Animal: _____   Flower: _____

What are some things this character doesn't like? _____

_____

What are some things this character is afraid of? _____

_____

Would you like this character for a friend? Why or why not? _____

_____

_____

CHANGES

People change from day to day, week to week and year to year. They learn from their mistakes, have new hopes and dreams. They have new responsibilities and worries.

Characters in books change, too. Select a character from a book or story you've read.

Character's name: _____

List words or phrases to describe what this character was like at the beginning of the story.

_____

_____

How did the character feel at the beginning of the story? _____

_____

_____

As the story continued, how did the character change? List words or phrases to describe the character at the middle of the story.

_____

_____

How did the character feel then? _____

_____

How did the character change by the end of the story? List words or phrases to describe the character at the end of the story.

_____

_____

How did the character feel at the end of the story? _____

_____

Compare the character at the beginning and end of the story. In what ways was the character the same? In what ways was the character different?

_____

_____

_____

_____

_____

_____

_____

_____

BEFORE AND AFTER

Select a book or story you've read. Answer the questions below.

Title: _____

Author: _____

Name of character: _____

Before the Story Began

Using what you know about the character, what do you think happened to this character before the story started?

_____

_____

_____

_____

Unanswered Questions

Sometimes stories end too soon. We have questions about what happened that aren't answered in the book. Write two questions you had about what happened to the character after the story ended.

1. _____

_____

2. _____

_____

After the Story

Explain what happened after the story ended by answering one of your questions.

_____

_____

_____

Would you like to read another story about this same character? Why or why not?

_____

_____

If the author decided to write another book about this character, what should the title be?

_____

◼ AROUND THE WORLD

Locate the city or country on the map where each book or story that you read takes place. Label the city or country and number it. On the numbered lines below, write the title of the book or story.

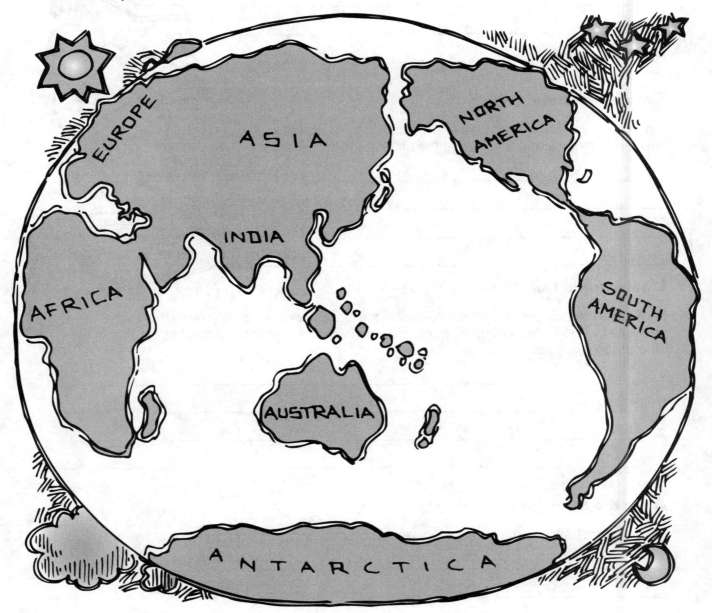

Write your book or story titles here:

1. _____   6. _____

2. _____   7. _____

3. _____   8. _____

4. _____   9. _____

5. _____   10. _____

HOME LIBRARY

Most families have quite a few books in their homes, usually more than they realize. What books do you and your family have at home? What magazines or newspapers does your family receive? Take an inventory of books you and your family own. List the titles and which family members read or use them.

Magazines and Newspapers:

_____

_____

Reference Books (dictionary, encyclopedia, atlas, etc.) (List the titles and type of book.):

_____

_____

Cookbooks:

_____

_____

_____

Manuals and "How to" Books:

_____

_____

Other Nonfiction Books:

_____

_____

Fiction Books (List titles and authors.):

_____

_____

_____

Rummage sales, library sales and used bookstores are great places to shop to add to your family library. List books, magazines and newspapers you would like to add to your family's home library.

_____

_____

_____

FINDING BOOKS

When you want to read more on a certain topic, use the library to find what's available. What sport or hobby are you interested in learning more about?

_____

Use the card catalog (or computer) at the library to find two books on this subject.

	Book 1	**Book 2**
Title	_____	_____
Author	_____	_____
Call number	_____	_____
Publisher	_____	_____
Date published	_____	_____
Fiction or Nonfiction	_____	_____

How many other books on this topic were listed in the card catalog? _____

Use the *Reader's Guide to Periodical Literature* to find one magazine article on your topic.

Article 1

Magazine	_____
Title of article	_____
Volume	_____
Date	_____
Page number	_____
Author (if given)	_____
Does your library carry this magazine?	_____

Describe two other sources you could check to find more information about your topic.

1. _____

2. _____

WHERE TO READ IT?

We read different types of books, newspapers and magazines to help us find different types of information. List the type or titles of books, magazines, newspapers or other sources where you could look to find . . .

Ideas to redecorate a room _____

Information about a rare stamp _____

The location of a city in Japan _____

A new recipe for macaroon cookies _____

Tomorrow's weather forecast _____

An unknown street in your city _____

Someone to mow the lawn _____

Instructions for building a birdhouse _____

A movie or book review _____

Directions to a nearby city _____

Directions to make a piñata _____

The best price on back-to-school clothes _____

Which movies are playing at the theater _____

Abraham Lincoln's middle name _____

The formula for the area of a circle _____

Someone's address _____

The population of Hawaii _____

The name of the Queen of England in 1856 _____

The meaning of *acrophobia* _____

The ingredients in Cheerios™ _____

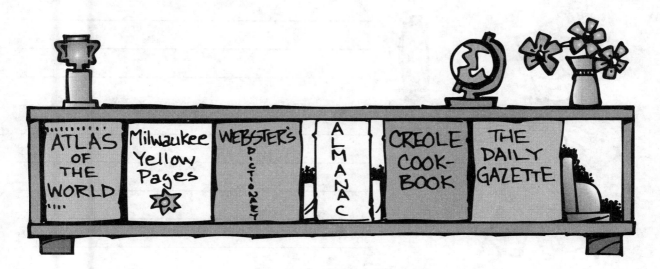

INVESTIGATOR, FIRST CLASS

Doing research is more fun if you are interested in the topic. For this activity you can investigate something you would like to know more about. Start by writing three questions on the lines below.

Examples:
- Why is the sky blue?
- How does popcorn pop?
- How do they get toothpaste into a tube?
- Why does Velcro™ stick?
- How do they get the lumps out of creamy peanut butter?
- Why do birds fly south in winter?

Your questions:

1. _____

2. _____

3. _____

Choose one of your questions. Gather information to answer the question. If you are having trouble finding the answer, ask your teacher or the librarian to suggest sources of information for your topic.

How did you go about finding the answer to your question? What sources did you use to find the information?

_____

_____

_____

What is the answer to your question? You may write your answer below, or present it in another way, like a chart, a graph, a poster or an illustration.

▥ READING NEWSPAPERS AND NEWS MAGAZINES

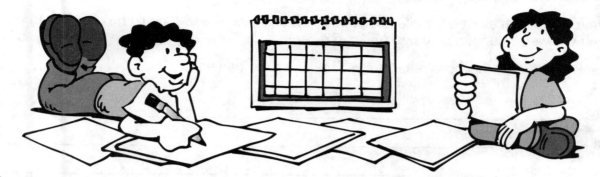

Select one day, any day since 1975 but not necessarily a "big news" day. Use at least three newspapers or news magazines (local, state and/or national) as sources.

Date: _____

Newspapers or magazines used: _____

_____

What were the top news headlines of the day?_____

_____

Who was President and Vice President on that day?_____

_____

List some type of medical news for that day. _____

_____

List four programs people could have watched on TV that day.

_____   _____

_____   _____

What movies could people have seen at the theater? Who starred in them?

_____

_____

List two problems or important issues of that day.

_____   _____

What was the weather like that day in your city? What was the weather "news" of the day?

_____

Read ads. List two products and their costs.

_____   _____

Discuss this statement: Today's newspapers are current events; yesterday's newspapers are history.

ALL-TIME FAVORITE

What is the best, all-time favorite book or story you've ever read? It could be one read to you when you were younger or one you've read recently.

If you haven't read this book recently, go back and read it again.

Title: _____

Author: _____

Main characters: _____

Describe your favorite character. _____

_____

Where does the story take place? _____

When does the story take place? _____

Write a short summary of the story. _____

_____

_____

_____

What's the best part of the story? _____

_____

_____

_____

Why does this book rate as your personal, all-time favorite?

_____

_____

_____

_____

_____

_____

_____

_____

_____

_____

◼▦ GOLDEN BOOK AWARD

Movies, actors and actresses receive awards called Emmys and Oscars. Musicians receive Grammy awards for songs and albums. Olympic winners receive gold, silver or bronze medals. Trophies, medals and ribbons are awarded for individual sports, team sports and car races. Even animals receive awards for being the best at something. Wouldn't it be appropriate to give out Golden Book Awards for the best books?

Design a Golden Book Award for the author of the best book you've ever read. Draw the award below. Include the title of the book and the author's name somewhere on the award.

What is the award made of? _____

_____

_____

Why did you choose this particular design? _____

_____

_____

LETTER TO AN AUTHOR

Have you ever wished you could talk to an author about a book or story you've read? Perhaps you have questions you'd like to ask. Do you wonder why the author wrote the book or why it ended that way? One way to find out would be to write a letter to an author. On another sheet of paper:

- Prewrite your letter by putting down some ideas.
- Tell the author a little about yourself.
- Explain why you liked the book.
- Write some questions you have about the author or the book.

Write the final draft of your letter neatly on another sheet of paper. Use this form for your letter. ➡

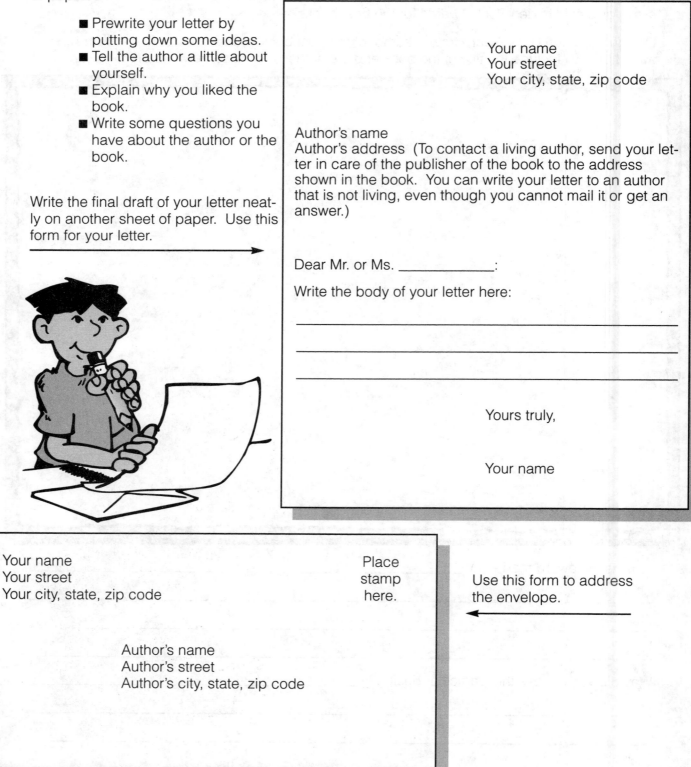

Your name
Your street
Your city, state, zip code

Author's name
Author's address (To contact a living author, send your letter in care of the publisher of the book to the address shown in the book. You can write your letter to an author that is not living, even though you cannot mail it or get an answer.)

Dear Mr. or Ms. _____:

Write the body of your letter here:

_____

_____

_____

Yours truly,

Your name

Your name
Your street
Your city, state, zip code

Place stamp here.

Use this form to address the envelope. ⬅

Author's name
Author's street
Author's city, state, zip code

▓ LETTER TO A CHARACTER

Have you ever wished you could talk to a character you've met in a book or story? Wouldn't it be nice to make friends with Charlie from the Chocolate Factory; Wilbur and Charlotte or Menolly, the Dragonsinger?

Select a character you'd like to get to know better. It could be a person or animal from any book or story you've read.

Character's name: _____

Title of book or story: _____

Jot down some ideas to use in your letter.

_____

What would you like to tell the character about yourself?

_____

_____

What are some things you have in common with this character?

_____

_____

Why did you decide to write to this character?

_____

_____

What do you admire about this character?

_____

_____

What are some questions you would like to ask this character?

_____

_____

Write the final draft of your letter neatly on another sheet of paper.

When you finish, "mail" the letter by writing the character's name and book title on the front of the envelope. Select one of the letters to another character written by a classmate. Write an answer to the letter and send it back.

▓ GOOD ADVICE

Would you like a job writing an advice column for a newspaper? The questions people ask cover every subject, from A to Z. Read several advice columns from your local newspaper.

Work with a partner. Select a character from a book or story you've both read. Think of some topic the character could use some advice about. On separate papers, you and your partner should write a question from the point of view of that character.

Character's name: _____

Book or story title: _____

Character's question:_____

_____

Dear Super Problem Solver,

_____

_____

_____

Signed,

_____

Trade papers and answer the question written by your partner.

Dear _____,

_____

_____

_____

Signed,

_____

▊▊ TALL TALES

Tall tales are stories about folk heroes who performed mighty deeds. Folk heroes could be real people like Johnny Appleseed or made-up heroes like Paul Bunyan. As the stories are retold, the tales get taller—that is, more exaggerated.

Hyperboles are figures of speech that use extreme exaggeration. "I'm hungry enough to eat an elephant" is hyperbole.

Finish each sentence below with a hyperbole.

I'm tired enough to _____

The wind blew so hard _____

The potholes in the road were so big _____

The smell from the bakery was so delicious, I _____

The snow was so deep _____

Last July it was so hot that _____

Read a book or story about a folk hero or character in a tall tale, then answer the questions below. Some folk heroes are:

- Paul Bunyan
- Captain Stormalong
- Daniel Boone
- Casey Jones
- Pecos Bill
- Mike Fink
- Johnny Appleseed
- Steamboat Bill
- John Henry
- Davy Crockett
- Joe Magarac

What does the character look like? _____

_____

How was he or she different than ordinary people?_____

_____

What great deeds did this character do?_____

_____

What was the hero's greatest achievement? _____

_____

Write three hyperboles about this character. You can use ones found in the story or make up your own.

_____

_____

_____

▓ A MODERN SUPER HERO

Here are examples of hyperboles (exaggerations) about folk heroes:

- When Paul Bunyan dug the lakes in Minnesota, he threw the dirt all the way to the Badlands of South Dakota.
- Davy Crockett won a wrestling match with a bear when he was three years old.
- Pecos Bill rode a panther and used a rattlesnake for a rope.

Imagine a modern super hero, one who lives in your neighborhood, belongs to your favorite pro sports team or goes to your school.

Fill in the information about your super hero below.

Name: _____

Physical description: _____

_____

Type of clothing worn: _____

_____

Talents or special abilities: _____

_____

_____

Pets or special friends (like Paul Bunyan and Babe the Blue Ox or Batman and Robin):

_____

_____

_____

Good deeds your super hero has done: _____

_____

_____

Great achievement: _____

_____

Write three hyperboles about your super hero.

_____

_____

_____

◧ FOUR SCENES

In the four panels below, draw four scenes from a book or story you've read. Below each drawing, write a short caption to explain the picture. Your drawing could be realistic or like a cartoon.

◼◼ SELL YOUR FAVORITE STORY

What's the best book or story you've read lately? _____
If you were a salesperson, how would you convince others to "buy" it?

Design an ad campaign to convince your classmates to read this book or story. Your sales plan should include an appeal to at least two of the senses: Hearing, sight, smell, taste, touch.

Here are some suggestions that you could use:

- Make up a jingle or two-line rhyming poem.

- Put your jingle to music.

- Make a sales poster.

- Make a travel brochure.

- Write a two-minute radio ad.

- Make something to give each classmate to help them remember the title and author.

- Draw a cartoon based on the story.

- Write a book review.

- Write a recipe inspired by the story.

- Dress up like a character in the story.

- Make decorations based on the story.

- Hand out free samples (a one-paragraph summary of why your classmates should read the story).

- Give a demonstration based on the story.

- Do a large painting, illustration or collage.

Use the space below to plan your sales campaign. Write your ideas and a first draft of your plan. Present your sales pitch to the class.

_____

_____

_____

_____

_____

_____

_____

■ A DOLLAR A WORD

When you read, look for the main idea of the story. The main idea can be stated in one or two sentences.

For example: A boy who is afraid of heights learns to overcome his fear. A girl discovers her best friend's dark secret.

Select a story you've read.

Title: _____

Write the main idea of the story below. Choose your words carefully. Don't waste words like "This book is about . . ."

Imagine that each word costs $1 and you have only $20 to spend.

_____ _____ _____ _____ _____

_____ _____ _____ _____ _____

_____ _____ _____ _____ _____

_____ _____ _____ _____

Now imagine you are writing a headline to summarize that same story. Headlines are very short. They usually contain a subject (the name of a person place or thing), a verb (an action word) and a direct object (another noun).

Look at the main idea you wrote above. Circle the subject, verb and direct object. Use them to write a headline for the story.

You have an even smaller budget this time—no more than $8.

For example: Boy Overcomes Fear of Heights
                Girl Discovers Friend's Secret

Write your headline.

_____

_____

Titles usually contain even less words than headlines. In this case, you may only use one word! It could be a word from your main idea or your headline. It could be any other word that summarizes the story or would make others want to read the story.

For example: Fear!
                Secrets

Write your title. _____

▐▌ BOARD GAMES

Monopoly® was invented during the Depression by a man who was out of work. People enjoyed buying and selling property and spending great sums of money at a time when most people had little real money to spend. Monopoly® streets are named for streets in Atlantic City, New Jersey, a vacation place the inventor had visited. Monopoly® has been translated into many languages and has remained the number one selling board game for many years.

You might not invent a game as popular as Monopoly®, but you can have fun inventing a board game that isn't boring. Your game can be as easy as Candyland® or Chutes and Ladders® or as difficult as Risk®. The only requirement is that the game must be based on a book or story you've read.

Work with a small group to come up with ideas for your game. Write your ideas below.

■ Book or story title: _____

Draw a small version of the board on another sheet of paper.

■ What is the object of the game? _____

_____

■ How many people can play this game? _____

■ What kind of markers do you need? How many do you need? What shape will they be? Describe them or draw them here:

■ Do you need dice or chips? How many? _____

■ Do you need a spinner? Draw it on the same piece of paper as the board game.

■ Do you need some type of cards for players to draw when they land on specific places or when they roll doubles? Give examples of at least 10 cards you will use.

■ Write the instructions for the game on a separate piece of paper.

■ As a team, work together to make a prototype of your game. Invite others to play. After playing the game, what changes could you make to improve the game?

_____

_____

_____

_____

_____

▦ I HAVE A DREAM

So I say to you, my friends, that even though we must face the difficulties of today and tomorrow, I still have a dream. It is a dream deeply rooted in the American dream that one day this nation will rise up and live out the true meaning of its creed—we hold these truths to be self-evident, that all men are created equal.

I have a dream that one day on the red hills of Georgia, sons of former slaves and sons of former slave-owners will be able to sit down together at the table of brotherhood.

I have a dream that one day, even the state of Mississippi, a state sweltering in the heat of injustice, sweltering with the heat of oppression, will be transformed into an oasis of freedom and justice.

I have a dream my four little children will one day live in a nation where they will not be judged by the color of their skin but by the content of their character. I have a dream today!

I have a dream that one day, down in Alabama, with its vicious racists . . . little black boys and black girls will be able to join hands with little white boys and white girls as sisters and brothers. I have a dream today!

I have a dream that one day every valley shall be exalted, every hill and mountain shall be made low, the rough places shall be made plain, and the crooked places shall be made straight and the glory of the Lord will be revealed and all flesh shall see it together. This is our hope. This is the faith that I go back to the South with.

With this faith we will be able to hew out of the mountain of despair a stone of hope. With this faith we will be able to transform the jangling discords of our nation into a beautiful symphony of brotherhood.

With this faith we will be able to work together, to pray together, to struggle together, to go to jail together, to stand up for freedom together, knowing that we will be free one day. This will be the day when all of God's children will be able to sing with new meaning—"my country 'tis of thee; sweet land of liberty; of thee I sing; land where my fathers died, land of the pilgrim's pride, from every mountain side, let freedom ring"—and if America is to be a great nation, this must become true.

So let freedom ring from the prodigious hilltops of New Hampshire.

Let freedom ring from the mighty mountains of New York.

Let freedom ring from the heightening Alleghenies of Pennsylvania.

Let freedom ring from the snow-capped Rockies of Colorado.

Let freedom ring from the curvaceous slopes of California.

But not only that.

Let freedom ring from Stone Mountain of Georgia.

Let freedom ring from Lookout Mountain of Tennessee.

DR. KING'S DREAM

Read the speech, "I Have a Dream" by Dr. Martin Luther King, Jr. given on August 28, 1963, in Washington, D.C.

Summarize Dr. King's dream in two or three sentences: _____

_____

_____

Explain in your own words what you think Dr. King meant by the phrases below. Refer to the speech as often as you wish.

"the table of brotherhood"

_____

_____

"Mississippi, a state sweltering in the heat of injustice"

_____

_____

"an oasis of freedom and justice"

_____

_____

a nation where people will be judged "by the content of their character . . ."

_____

_____

"to hew out of the mountain of despair a stone of hope"

_____

_____

"transform the jangling discords of our nation into a beautiful symphony of brotherhood"

_____

_____

"Let freedom ring"

_____

_____

Why do you think this speech became famous?

_____

_____

◼ YOUR DREAM

What dream do you have for the future? List words and phrases that describe your dream.

_____   _____

_____   _____

_____   _____

_____   _____

_____   _____

_____   _____

Write a short speech based on your dream.

I Have a Dream

_____

_____

_____

_____

_____

_____

_____

_____

_____

_____

_____

_____

Compare and contrast your speech to Dr. King's. How is your dream similar to Dr. King's? In what ways are they different?

ACTIVITIES AND DISCUSSION TOPICS

Discussion Topics

■ Many people give speeches, but few are remembered for long. Why is Dr. King's "I Have a Dream" speech still famous?

■ Why do you think this speech was effective?

■ What sources did Dr. King quote from in his speech?

■ Who do you think was more affected by Dr. King's speech, whites or African Americans? Why?

■ What is your favorite phrase in the speech? Why?

Complete the assigned activities from the list below.

1. Memorize the last eight lines of the speech and deliver them with enthusiasm.

2. Practice reading the speech out loud. Give the speech to the class.

3. Underline 10 words in the speech that may not be clear to you. Write definitions for these words.

4. Read several articles from newspapers or news magazines about Dr. King's speech. Summarize the articles.

5. Find quotes from news sources regarding people's opinion of this speech.

6. Write an essay question that could be used on a test about Dr. King's speech. Answer the question.

7. Write a report about Dr. Martin Luther King, Jr.'s life.

8. Write a report about the Civil Rights Movement in the early 1960s.

9. Write a report about the Civil Rights Movement today.

10. Watch a tape of Dr. King giving his speech. Write your impressions of his delivery of the speech.

11. Do an illustration of the future when Dr. King's dream has come true.

12. Make a collage representing Dr. King's dream.

DEAR MR. HENSHAW

Read *Dear Mr. Henshaw* by Beverly Cleary.

About the Author: Beverly Cleary grew up in Oregon. After graduating from the University of California—Berkeley, she earned a second degree in Librarianship from the University of Washington in Seattle. She became a children's librarian in Yakima, Washington. She and her husband moved to California in 1949.

Ms. Cleary was born in 1916 but did not begin writing her first book, *Henry Huggins*, until 1950. She is the mother of twins, now grown.

Beverly Cleary has earned many awards for her writing including the Laura Ingalls Wilder Award, the 1980 Regina Medal and the University of Southern Mississippi's 1982 Silver Medallion. *Ramona and Her Father* and *Ramona Quimby, Age 8* were named Newbery Medal winners and her book, *Dear Mr. Henshaw*, won the 1984 Newbery Medal.

Discussion Topics

- Leigh feels the divorce might be his fault. Why? Do you think it was his fault? Why or why not?

- Why was Leigh glad he had stopped the lunch box thief without catching him or her?

- How do you think authors feel about getting letters from readers?

- Do you think Leigh will continue to write letters to Mr. Henshaw?

- From the time his second grade teacher read it to the class, Ways to Amuse a Dog became Leigh's favorite book. He read it over and over. Do you have a book or story you've enjoyed reading many times or a movie you've watched over and over? What is special about it?

- Leigh's dad said he'd call but usually didn't. How did that make Leigh feel?

- Sometimes adults do not keep their promises. How does this make you feel?

- How did you like reading a book written as letters and in journal form? Was it easy to follow the plot?

- What did you think of the ending of this book?

Other Reading

Some other books by Beverly Cleary include *Beezus and Ramona*, *Ramona the Pest*, *The Mouse and the Motorcycle*, *Henry and Ribsy*, *Runaway Ralph* and *Socks*.

▌▓ BIG EVENTS

While he was in sixth grade, many important events took place in Leigh's life. His parents got a divorce. He moved to a new house in a new city. He started at a new school. He lost his dog. He won honorable mention in the Young Writer's contest.

Which event in Leigh's life do you think affected him the most? Why?

_____

_____

_____

New Kid in School

Leigh is lonely. He misses his dad and Bandit. His mother is often away at work or class. Leigh hasn't made any friends at his new school.

What are some ways you could help a new classmate feel welcome?

_____

_____

_____

Lunch Box Alarm

Leigh rigged up a lunch box alarm using a battery and a doorbell. Design another type of lunch box or lunch bag alarm. Write an explanation or draw a diagram to show how it would work.

_____

_____

_____

Dear Journal

Read a page from the early part of Leigh's journal. Compare it to a page towards the end of the book. How does Leigh's writing change?

_____

Write your own journal entry on another page.

CHANGES

List four ways Leigh changed from the beginning of sixth grade until the end of the book.

_____

_____

_____

_____

Leigh and His Dad

Did Leigh's dad change from the beginning of the book until the end? Explain.

_____

_____

What did you learn about truck driving? Do you think all truck drivers are as irresponsible as Leigh's dad?

_____

_____

Why do you think Leigh felt so terrible when he called his dad and heard another boy's voice in the background?

_____

_____

Leigh had mixed feelings about his dad. Explain how Leigh could love and miss his dad, and at the same time, feel angry and sometimes even think he hated his father.

_____

_____

Do you think Leigh's mother had mixed feelings about his father, too? Explain.

_____

_____

▉ SO, HOW'S SCHOOL?

"You've grown," he said, which is what grown-ups always say when they don't know what else to say to kids.

"How do you like school?" is another question adults seem to ask, just for something to say.

What are some things adults say to you when they don't know what to say?

_____

_____

_____

_____

Why do you think adults have trouble talking to kids?

_____

_____

_____

_____

What questions do you wish adults would ask and really listen to the answers?

_____

_____

What's a Grandfather?

Leigh says, "I wish I had a grandfather like Mr. Fridley. He is so nice, sort of baggy and comfortable."

How do you picture a grandfather? Write a short description.

_____

_____

_____

What is your idea of a grandmother?

_____

_____

LONELINESS IS ONE SHOE BY THE SIDE OF THE ROAD

A metaphor is a figure of speech that compares two unlike items without using the words *like* or *as*.

Here are some examples:

- Happiness is a surprise visit from someone special.
- Loneliness is listening to the ping, ping from the gas station.
- Amazement is millions of monarchs on the butterfly trees.

Fill in the blanks to complete the metaphors.

Loneliness is _____

Happiness is _____

Sadness is _____

Anger is _____

Contentment is _____

Security is _____

Write two metaphors of your own.

_____

_____

Adjectives

An **adjective** is a word that describes a noun. *Happy, lonely, pretty, green* and *medium* are adjectives.

List five adjectives that describe Leigh's mother.	List five adjectives that describe Leigh's dad.
1. _____	_____
2. _____	_____
3. _____	_____
4. _____	_____
5. _____	_____

List adjectives that describe Leigh.

▌WHAT DID THEY MEAN?

Read the following sentences from the book. Explain what you think the characters meant.

Leigh's mother says, "It takes two people to get a divorce."

_____

_____

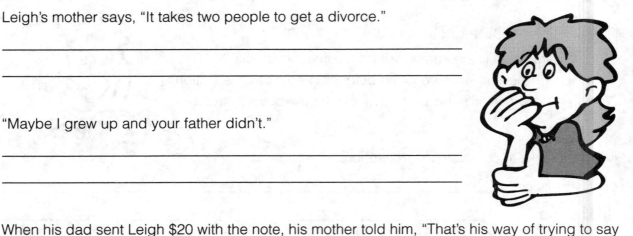

"Maybe I grew up and your father didn't."

_____

_____

When his dad sent Leigh $20 with the note, his mother told him, "That's his way of trying to say he really is sorry about Bandit."

_____

_____

Leigh misses his dog and wishes he were there to keep him company. After all, "Bandit and I didn't get a divorce. They did."

_____

_____

When Leigh went to get the supplies for the lunch box alarm, he noticed someone watching him. "Boys my age always get watched when they go into stores."

_____

_____

Mr. Fridley told Leigh that everybody has problems, if you take the trouble to notice.

_____

_____

At the end of the book, Leigh says, "I felt sad and a whole lot better at the same time."

_____

_____

▚ THIMBLE SUMMER

Read *Thimble Summer* by Elizabeth Enright.

About the Author: Elizabeth Enright is considered an outstanding writer of realistic fiction and fantasy for children. The children in her books live in families who supply lots of love and mutual support. She stresses the joys of childhood more than the conflicts and pain of growing up. In writing *Thimble Summer*, the author drew on her experiences during one summer on her uncle's farm and from stories her mother and grandmother told about their childhood. *Thimble Summer* won the 1939 Newbery Medal Award.

Discussion Topics

■ Would you have liked to live in Wisconsin in the 1930s? Why or why not?

■ Would you like to spend a summer living on a farm? Why or why not?

■ To Garnet, the library was a friendly, familiar place until she and Citronella were locked in at night. Then how did they feel about the library?

■ How would you feel if you were locked in a store or a library overnight?

■ Why do some places seem more scary at night?

■ When Mr. Linden brought Eric home to live with them, Mrs. Linden welcomed him. How do you think your parents would have reacted to Eric?

■ "Mrs. Linden was the mother of three children and hardly anything surprised her any more." What does that mean?

■ Do you think Eric continued to live with the Lindens? Why or why not?

■ What do you think of the title of this book?

■ What are some other possible titles for it?

Other Reading

Other books by Elizabeth Enright include *Intu: A Congo Adventure, The Sea Is All Around, Zeee, Tatsinda, The Saturdays, The Four-Story Mistake, Then There Were Five* and *Spiderweb for Two.*

◼▦ SIMILES

A simile is a figure of speech that compares two unlike objects using the words *like* or *as*.

Here are some similes found in *Thimble Summer*:

- "His hair hung to his head like wet feathers and his cheeks were as red as radishes."
- Garnet saw "a snake move like a drawn ribbon through wet ferns."
- "You look like a hen with a stomachache," Jay told Garnet.
- ". . . the corn on the hillside was like a parade advancing with plumes and banners."
- Garnet describes riding in their old Ford as ". . . rather like being on a throne, and rather like being in a motorboat."
- The door of the kiln was "red-hot and glowing like the eye of a dragon."
- Even when he was asleep, Mr. Freebody's mustache ". . . looked as though it were awake and keeping watch."
- When they were threshing, Garnet says Mr. Freebody ". . . looked like an old walrus that had got mixed up with some seaweed."

Find two other examples of similes from the book.

1. _____

2. _____

How does the use of similes make this story more interesting?

_____

_____

Complete the sentences below with your own similes.

When Timmy won the blue ribbon, Garnet felt as proud as . . .

_____

Mr. Freebody's big, bushy mustache looked like . . .

_____

The big, ripe watermelons were like . . .

_____

After Garnet fell in the mud puddle, she looked like . . .

_____

The chickens took off in all directions like . . .

_____

SOUNDS ALL AROUND

Stop and listen for one minute. What do you hear?

_____

Listen again. People get so used to sounds around them that they tune them out. What else do you hear?

_____

The author makes us aware of the sounds Garnet hears.

- Garnet wore a pair of Jay's rubber boots that made a "slumph, slumph noise at every step."
- "The thunder was like big drums, like cannons, like the Fourth of July, only louder."

Describe some sounds by completing the sentences below.

The thunder was like . . .

_____

The hens squawked like . . .

_____

The wind sounded like . . .

_____

The crash of the waves on the rocky shore was like . . .

_____

Descriptive Writing

Here are some other examples of descriptive writing found in *Thimble Summer*:

- "The teapot smiled all around its lid and purred like a kitten . . ."
- ". . . the alarm clock stood with feet apart and wore its little gong like a cap on top . . ."
- The watermelons in their patch were little green whales in a sea of frothy leaves . . ."

Select one of these examples or another one from the book. Explain what it means and how it adds to the story.

SMELLS

- "The Hauser house had its own smell like all houses. It smelled of brown soap and ironing and linoleum: rather stuffy."
- "Garnet loved the library; it smelled deliciously of old books . . ."
- "There were hundreds of odors in the night air: Garnet raised her nose like a puppy to smell them all."

Describe the odors you would smell . . .

in the country:

_____

_____

in a large city:

_____

_____

at a zoo:

_____

_____

at a movie theater:

_____

_____

at a mall:

_____

_____

The cornfields ". . . had a special smell after dark that you never noticed in the daytime." How can things smell different after dark than they do when it's light?

_____

_____

_____

How do descriptions of smells make a story more interesting?

_____

_____

ONE OF THOSE DAYS

In Chapter V Garnet says, "It had been one of those dull, dull days when nothing interesting happens and everything goes wrong. It was the kind of day that you stub your toe a lot and lose things, and forget what it was that your mother asked you to get at the store."

Describe a day you've had that was "one of those days."

_____
_____
_____
_____
_____
_____
_____
_____
_____
_____

Stories Within a Story

Some authors tell stories within the story, stories told by a minor character.

Eric told the story about how he lived before he met the Lindens.

Citronella's great-great grandmother told stories to Garnet and Citronella. Ask your oldest grandparent or neighbor to tell you a story about something he or she did at your age. Write the story below and illustrate it on a separate piece of paper.

_____
_____
_____
_____
_____
_____
_____
_____

WHAT DO YOU THINK?

Do you think Jay and Garnet were expected to do too much work around the farm? Why or why not?

_____

_____

How do you feel when the weather has been hot and sticky for a long time?

_____

_____

How do you think Garnet felt about Eric?

_____

_____

How did Garnet feel when Jay and Eric began spending time together and excluding her?

_____

_____

_____

Although he wasn't related to her, Mr. Freebody always looked out for Garnet. Why?

_____

_____

_____

Why do you think Garnet ran away after she had the fight with Jay in Chapter VI?

_____

_____

_____

"I'm never going to be too old for the merry-go-round," Garnet says. "All my life whenever I see a merry-go-round I'm going to ride on it, and when I have children I'm going to ride with them." Do you think Garnet will ride on a merry-go-round when she grows up? Why or why not?

_____

_____

"It was a good thing that Eric had taught her to do handsprings and flip-ups, Garnet decided. It was very handy to know how to do one or two when you felt happy." Why?

_____

_____

TOO MUCH MAGIC

Read *Too Much Magic* by Betsy and Sam Sterman.

Discussion Topics

■ Is it better to have had magic and lost it, than never to have had it at all?

■ After Jeff demonstrates the wishing cube: "'Wow' I said again. It was all I could think of to say, but it expressed everything." What did Bill mean?

■ How could a wishing cube be dangerous?

■ What did you think of the illustrations for this story?

■ Was this story realistic? Could something like this happen in real life? Why or why not?

■ What do you think this saying means? If wishes were horses then beggars could ride.

■ If you had been Bill or Jeff, what would you have done differently?

■ If you could have made one wish on the wishing cube, what would it be? Think carefully about the wording before making your wish.

■ Making wishes is easy. Controlling them can be complicated and sometimes even dangerous. Why?

Other Reading

From the Mixed-Up Files of Mrs. Basil E. Frankweiler by E.L. Konigsburg.

Freaky Friday by Mary Rogers.

Half Magic by Edward Eager.

THE WISHING CUBE

Why do you think the authors chose to tell the story from Bill's point of view?

_____

_____

When his dad saw the motorbike, Bill said, "Our dad's a good-natured guy and fair about most things, but this was too much for him." What did Bill mean?

_____

_____

What do you suppose his parents would have said if Jeff had told them about the wishing cube?

_____

_____

What do you suppose they would have done if Jeff had demonstrated the wishing cube?

_____

_____

Why didn't it work when the boys wished for another wishing cube?

_____

_____

"We had decided to keep the cube a secret from everybody, even our best friends." Why did Jeff and Bill keep the wishing cube a secret?

_____

Why would it be difficult to keep a secret like that for very long?

_____

_____

Were you disappointed when you found out the wishing cube wasn't magic? Why or why not?

_____

_____

_____

_____

HINTS OF WHAT WILL HAPPEN

In many places in the story, events and dialogue occur that predict other events later in the story. Read these statements from the book. How did they turn out as predictions for what finally happened?

In Chapter 2, Bill tells Jeff, "You can't always have everything your own way."

_____

_____

Bill says that magic is "okay for a little kid like Jeff, but I don't believe in magic. In the real world there isn't any such thing."

_____

_____

"The power company's been having a lot of trouble lately . . ."

_____

_____

"Was there . . . could there possibly be any sort of connection between the jogger and the cube?"

_____

_____

Bill says: ". . . I began to wonder if having this cube could mean trouble—big trouble."

_____

_____

_____

"It's too risky to do any more wishing till we can handle it better."

_____

_____

_____

Coach said that he wished he could scare some sense into Jeff.

_____

_____

_____

A WRINKLE IN TIME

Read *A Wrinkle in Time* by Madeleine L'Engle.

About the Author: Born in New York City in 1918, Madeleine L'Engle was an only child brought up with a nanny and a governess. As a child she developed a great love of reading and writing stories. For a time, her family moved to Switzerland where she attended boarding school. Ms. L'Engle has published more than 40 books. Her best-known book, *A Wrinkle in Time*, won the 1962 Newbery Medal. She has written science fiction, suspense, young adult novels, plays and nonfiction books. Many of her books show her concern for a happy family life and the right of individuals to make choices.

Other Reading

A Wind in the Door, A Swiftly Tilting Planet, The Moon by Night, The Arm of the Starfish, Dragons in the Water, The Young Unicorns, Meet the Austins and *Dance in the Desert* by Madeleine L'Engle.

"Mrs. Todd's Shortcut" by Stephen King.

"And He Built a Crooked House" by Robert Heinlein.

Chapter by Chapter

Chapter 1

Define the words listed before you read each chapter. Use a dictionary if needed. Answer the questions after you finish each chapter.

Chapter 1. Mrs. Whatsit

> constable
> delinquent
> exclusive
> frenzied
> scudded
> tesseract
> wardrobe

How did Meg feel about herself in the opening scene?

_____

What do we learn about Meg's brother, Charles Wallace?

_____

How does the author build suspense in the first chapter?

_____

▉ CHAPTER BY CHAPTER

Chapters 2 and 3

Chapter 2. Mrs. Who

antagonistic	belligerent	compulsion	dilapidated
disillusion	flounced	inadvertently	inexcusably
piteous	raucous	sinister	tractable

The second chapter raises many questions but answers none. List several questions you have after reading this chapter.

_____

_____

The principal, Mr. Jenkins tells Meg she should be less antagonistic. How is Meg antagonistic? How is Mr. Jenkins antagonistic?

_____

_____

Chapter 3. Mrs. Which

autumnal	decipher	dubiously	gamboled
judiciously	morass	sullen	wafted

Why do you think Mrs. Who quotes from different people in different languages? Select one of her quotations and explain how it fits the scene.

_____

_____

Meg asks her mother, "Do you think things always have an explanation?" Explain her mother's reply.

_____

_____

Meg is a very angry girl. Explain why she is so angry.

_____

_____

CHAPTER BY CHAPTER

Chapters 4 and 5

Chapter 4. The Black Thing

comprehensible	condensed	corona	corporeal
dispersed	elliptic	ephemeral	extinguished
extraordinary	fragment	frenzy	ineffable
materialize	metamorphose	monolith	obscure
resonant	tangible	unobscured	verbalize

How would you feel if you were suddenly whisked off to a faraway planet by three people you hardly knew?

_____

_____

_____

Mrs. Whatsit tries to explain how they travel. "We tesser. Or you might say, we wrinkle." Calvin says that explanation is "Clear as mud." What does he mean?

_____

_____

_____

_____

Chapter 5. The Tesseract

coursed	dissolution	indignant
intolerable	nondescript	protoplasm
reverberated	sonorous	subsided

What do you think it means when the Happy Medium cries at the end of the chapter?

_____

_____

_____

Mrs. Whatsit says, "Explanations are not easy when they are about things for which your civilization still has no words." She then tries again to explain the fifth dimension and how they travel. Rewrite her explanation in your own words as you understand it.

_____

_____

_____

◼ CHAPTER BY CHAPTER

Chapters 6 and 7

Chapter 6. The Happy Medium

anticlimax	arrogance	distressed	faltered	identical
malignant	medium	myopic	propitious	seethe
solidity	talisman	unkempt	vulnerable	writhe

Mrs. Whatsit was once a star. What do you think happened to her?

_____

_____

How would you like to live in a place like Camazotz where all the houses were identical and all the people did the same things at the same time?

_____

_____

Chapter 7. The Man with Red Eyes

bilious	bravado	chinks	chortling	dilated
diverting	dogged	gallivanting	hypnotize	neurological
recourse	tenacity	unsubstantial	vocalize	

At the end of this chapter, Meg shrieks, "That isn't Charles! Charles is gone!" What does she mean? Where do you think Charles went?

_____

_____

CHAPTER BY CHAPTER

Chapters 8, 9 and 10

Chapter 8. The Transparent Column

annihilate	connotation	emanate	henchmen
infuriated	misconception	monotonous	ominous
pedantic	pinioned	primitive	sadist
somber	sulphurous	transparent	wryly

Meg says, "Maybe if you aren't unhappy sometimes you don't know how to be happy . . ."
Do you agree or disagree? Explain your answer.

_____

_____

Chapter 9. It

artificial	cerebellum	cerebrum	dais	disembodied
endurance	gibberish	groping	impenetrable	inexorable
nauseating	placidly	sniggered	zombie	

Charles Wallace explains that on Camazotz everyone is equal because everyone is the same
as everybody else. Meg realizes that *like* and *equal* are two entirely different things. Explain.

_____

_____

Chapter 10. Absolute Zero

assuaged	atrophy	corrosive	disintegration
fallible	loathing	paralyzed	revulsion

This chapter is titled "Absolute Zero." What does *absolute zero* mean?

_____

_____

▌CHAPTER BY CHAPTER

Chapters 11 and 12

Chapter 11. Aunt Beast

distraught   gorge   perplexity   trepidation

Meg tries to explain *light* and *sight* to creatures that have no
eyes. She doesn't do very well. How would you explain these
words to someone like Aunt Beast?

_____

_____

Although Aunt Beast and her people are very strange looking to Meg, she trusts them. Why?

_____

_____

Chapter 12. The Foolish and the Weak

exuberance   formidable   reiterating   singularly   unadulterated

What does Meg have that IT doesn't have? How does this save her baby brother?

_____

_____

At the end of the book, Mrs. Whatsit starts to explain why they are in a hurry. Finish her sentence: "You see, we have too—"

_____

_____

How has Meg changed since the beginning of the book?

_____

_____

How do you think Meg and Charles Wallace will get along now?

_____

_____

What do you think happens to the friendship between Calvin, Meg and Charles Wallace?

_____

_____

 OTHER ACTIVITIES

Other Activities

Complete the assigned activities.

- Illustrate one of the characters from *A Wrinkle in Time*.

- Illustrate one of the places Meg visits.

- In *A Wrinkle in Time* you met Mrs. Whatsit, Mrs. Who and Mrs. Which. Describe another character that might have been a friend of theirs: Mrs. How, Mrs. When, Mrs. Where or Mrs. Why.

- The characters list several people who have fought the dark evil: Jesus, Leonardo da Vinci, Michelangelo, Shakespeare, Bach, Pasteur, Madame Curie, Einstein, Schweitzer, Gandhi, Buddha, Beethoven, Rembrandt, St. Francis, Euclid and Copernicus. Explain what one of these people did to fight evil. What other names could you add to this list?

- Charles Wallace is overcome by IT because he believes he is strong enough and smart enough to resist. "Pride goeth before a fall," is an old saying. How does this apply to Charles Wallace?

- What are some of Meg's faults? How do her faults help her?

- Describe what it might be like to live on a two-dimensional planet.

- Describe what it might be like to live on a four- or five-dimensional planet.

- How is Charles Wallace different than most five-year-olds? Compare Charles Wallace to Peter Hatcher's five-year-old brother Fudge, in *Fudge-A-Mania* by Judy Blume.

Discussion Topics

- How are Meg and Charles Wallace alike?

- Would you like to have a little brother like Charles Wallace? Why or why not?

- Which of the three Mrs. Ws would you most like to meet—Mrs. Whatsit, Mrs. Who or Mrs. Which? Why?

- Meg's mother tells her that people are more than just the way they look. Do you agree? Why or why not?

- What do you think of Meg's mother? Would you like to have a mother like her? Why or why not?

- The Happy Medium says, "It's my worst trouble, getting fond. If I didn't get fond I could be happy all the time." How can getting fond of people make us unhappy?

- "Love conquers all." How does this saying relate to the book?

- Did you like this book? Why or why not?

◼▦ THE LORAX

Read *The Lorax* by Dr. Seuss.

About the Author: Theodore Seuss Geisel, better known as Dr. Seuss, wrote and illustrated more than 50 children's books that make use of tongue-twisting rhymes, made-up words and simple illustrations. Many of his stories, like *The Lorax, Horton Hatches the Egg* and *The Sneetches* have subtle messages or morals. As a cartoonist, Dr. Seuss used the pen name, Theo Le Seig.

Discussion Topics

◼ Why does the Once-ler always stay out of sight?

◼ Whose rights are more important: the right of the Once-ler and his family to run a business and make money or the rights of the Truffula Trees, the Brown Bar-ba-loots, the Swomee-Swans and the Humming-Fish? Why?

◼ What else could the Lorax have done to stop the Once-ler from chopping down the Truffula Trees?

◼ Who lifted the Lorax and took him away? Why? Will he come back?

◼ Who was the winner in this story? Who was the loser? Why?

◼ Why did cutting down the Truffula Trees hurt the Brown Bar-ba-loots, the Swomee-Swans and the Humming-Fish?

◼ The Lorax tried to stop the Once-ler, but the Once-ler didn't listen. How did the Once-ler feel at the end of the story?

◼ If you were the Lorax, what would you have done or said to the Once-ler?

◼ If you were the Once-ler, what would you have done or said to the Lorax?

◼ What does the word *Unless* mean at the end of the story?

Write your answer to one of the above questions.

_____

_____

_____

_____

Other Reading

Other favorite books by Dr. Seuss include *The Cat in the Hat; How the Grinch Stole Christmas* and *Oh, the Places You'll Go!*

Going Green: A Kid's Handbook to Saving the Planet by John Elkington, Julia Hailes, Douglas Hill and Joel Makower (Puffin Books, 1990).

Fifty Simple Things Kids Can Do to Save the Earth by The Earth Works Group (Andrews & McMeel, 1990).

▦ NEED OR WANT?

The Once-ler says that everyone NEEDS a Thneed. Think about the difference between things we NEED and things we WANT.

After each word, circle NEED or WANT. Tell why you gave your answer.

1. Food   NEED   WANT

_____

_____

2. Candy   NEED   WANT

_____

_____

3. Television   NEED   WANT

_____

_____

4. Shelter   NEED   WANT

_____

_____

5. Car   NEED   WANT

_____

_____

6. Fur coat   NEED   WANT

_____

_____

7. Clothing   NEED   WANT

_____

_____

8. Stereo   NEED   WANT

_____

_____

9. Vegetables   NEED   WANT

_____

_____

10. Money   NEED   WANT

_____

_____

SETTING THE TONE

Read the first page of *The Lorax* very carefully. How does the description of the Street of the Lifted Lorax make you feel? List some words that describe those feelings.

_____   _____   _____

_____   _____   _____

_____   _____   _____

To set the tone for a happy story, list some words you could use.

_____   _____   _____

_____   _____   _____

_____   _____   _____

To set the tone for a sad story, list some words you could use.

_____   _____   _____

_____   _____   _____

_____   _____   _____

Unless

You have just been given the last Truffula Tree seed by the Once-ler. What will you do now? Write or draw your answer below.

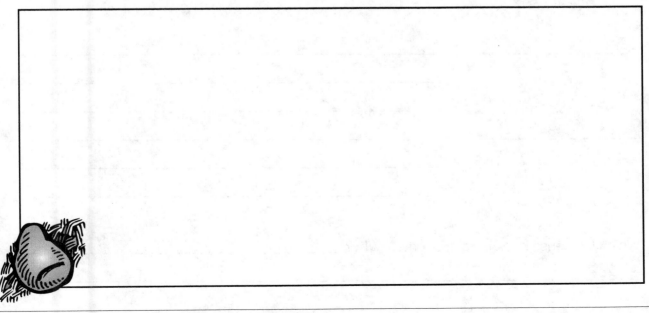

WORDS THAT AREN'T

Dr. Seuss uses many made-up words. Some examples are *snergelly, snarggled, cruffulous, smogulous, glumping, smoke-smuggered.* Find these words in the story. Write a definition for each of these made-up words:

SNERGELLY _____

SNARGGLED _____

CRUFFULOUS _____

SMOGULOUS _____

GLUMPING _____

SMOKE-SMUGGERED _____

Make up some of your own words. What do they mean?

Your made-up words: What they mean:

_____   _____

                        _____

                        _____

_____   _____

                        _____

                        _____

Which Dr. Seuss book is your favorite? Why? _____

_____

ONOMATOPOEIA

A word or group of words that imitates a sound is called an *onomatopoeia*. Dr. Seuss uses several made-up words like *ga-Zump, whiffed, snarggled, Gluppity-Glupp, sawdusty sneeze* and *Schloppity-Schlopp*.

Write words or groups of words that imitate the sounds listed below. You can use real words or made-up words.

The sound of the wind on a dark, cold night:

_____

The sound made when you pull the plug in a bathtub or sink:

_____

The sound of an apple falling from a tree:

_____

The sound of a sneeze in a hollow log:

_____

The sound of raindrops or snow:

_____

The sound of happy people:

_____

The sound of the last Truffula Tree as it falls:

_____

The sound of an animal laughing:

_____

Select one of these activities to complete:

- We never see a picture of the Once-ler, only parts of him. Draw a picture of what you think the Once-ler looks like.

- How are Brown Bar-ba-loots like grizzly bears or sea otters? How are Swamee-Swans like peregrine falcons, trumpeter swans or California condors? How are Humming-Fish like grey whales? Many plants and animals have become endangered because of the actions of people.

- Find information on one type of endangered animal, how it became endangered and what is being done to save the animals from extinction.

ISLAND OF THE BLUE DOLPHINS

Read *Island of the Blue Dolphins* by Scott O'Dell.

About the Author: Scott O'Dell, one of the best-known writers of historical fiction for children, was born in Los Angeles and is considered an authority on California history. Although he attended several colleges, he never completed a formal degree. He worked as a motion picture cameraman and a book editor for a Los Angeles newspaper before becoming a full-time writer in 1934.

Mr. O'Dell won the 1961 Newbery Medal Award for his book *Island of the Blue Dolphins* which was based on a true story. Three of his other books have been Newbery Honor books. He has won many other awards including the Hans Christian Andersen Award for lifetime achievement in 1972.

Matching

Write the letter of the correct answer in each blank.

1. _____ Ulape
2. _____ Chowig
3. _____ Ramo
4. _____ Won-a-pa-lei
5. _____ Kimki
6. _____ Orlov
7. _____ Ghalas-at
8. _____ Rontu
9. _____ Tutok
10. _____ Mon-a-nee

A. Karana's pet dog
B. The name of the village
C. Karana's sister
D. Girl with the Long Black Hair
E. Karana's father
F. Chief who sails looking for new home
G. The sea otter
H. Karana's brother
I. Aleutian girl who befriends Karana
J. Russian leader

Discussion Topics

- Why were Karana's father and the other villagers suspicious of Captain Orlov and the Aleuts?

- Do you think Karana was lonely or content most of the time?

- Was Karana a very brave girl or a very foolish one? Use specific incidents in the story to justify your answer.

- Karana could have hidden when the ship came at the end of the book. Why didn't she?

- Do you think the decision to leave the island with the strangers was easy or difficult? Why?

- What do you think it would be like to live all alone on an island for 18 years?

- What do you learn about this story by reading the Author's Notes at the end of the book?

Other Reading

Other books by Scott O'Dell include *The Black Pearl*, *The King's Fifth*, *Sing Down the Moon*, *Carlota*, *The Road to Damietta*, *Streams to the River, River to the Sea*, *Black Star, Bright Dawn* and *Zia*, a sequel to *Island of the Blue Dolphins*.

◼️▦ WHAT DO YOU THINK?

Why does Karana jump overboard? Was it a brave or foolish act?

_____

Did Karana have a good reason why she allowed her brother to go off alone to get the canoe? Explain your answer.

_____

Karana felt very sad about her brother's death, but she did not seem to blame herself. Why?

_____

Why do you think Karana burned the houses in the village?

_____

Why do you think she did not want to live there?

_____

Karana starts off in the canoe to find the land to the east. Why did she turn back?

_____

What would you have done?

_____

At the beginning of Chapter 11, Karana says she is "glad to be home." Why do you think she was glad?

_____

Karana could have repaired the canoe and tried again to sail for the lands to the east but decides not to try. "Now I knew that I would never go again." Why?

_____

Karana was not afraid to face the wild dogs or the sea elephants. Why do you think she was afraid to meet the Aleut girl?

_____

Why do you think the Aleut girl didn't tell the others that Karana was on the island?

_____

At the end of Chapter 23, Karana describes how she wore her necklace, earrings and cormorant feather dress and walked along the cliff with Rontu. Why do you think she would dress up when there was no one to see her?

_____

DIFFICULT DECISIONS

Karana knows it is forbidden for women to make weapons. Even though there is no one to see her, it takes several days for her to decide to break the taboo. Why?

_____

Karana didn't know how to make weapons. "I had watched, but not with the eye of one who would ever do it." What does that mean?

_____

At the end of the book, Karana decided to leave with the strangers. Do you think this was an easy decision? Why or why not?

_____

How Did They Live?

At the beginning of Chapter 7 Karana describes what she is packing to take with her on the ship. What does this tell you about how she and her people lived?

_____

_____

_____

Other Activities

Complete one of the activities listed below.

- Illustrate the fence of whalebones or the home Karana builds as it is described in Chapter 12.
- Label these places on a world map: Russia, the Bering Sea, the Aleutian Islands, Alaska, California, Santa Catalina and San Nicolas. How far is it from Russia to the Aleutian Islands? How far from the Aleutian Islands (where the Aleuts lived) to San Nicolas (the Island of the Blue Dolphins)? How far from San Nicolas to the nearest land?
- Select one of the animals or birds from the story for a report.   Describe what the animals look like, where they live, how large they grow, what they eat, etc.
- Write a description of what Karana's life was like after she left the Island of the Blue Dolphins.

KARANA AND THE ANIMALS

Why does Karana declare war on the wild dogs, especially their leader?

_____

Why does she save the wounded dog?

_____

After Rontu dies, Karana decides to trap another dog. Why? She has a specific dog in mind. Why?

_____

Reread the description of a devilfish. By what name do we know this animal?

_____

Was Karana brave when she decided to try to kill a bull sea elephant with a bow and arrow or was she foolish? How large is a bull sea elephant? Do you think she would have succeeded?

_____

_____

Why did Karana take care of many animals, feed them and keep them around her?

_____

After making friends with many animals, Karana decides never to kill another one, not even a wild dog. Why?

_____

Do you think Karana would have felt the same if she hadn't been stranded alone on the island? Why or why not?

_____

_____

Karana says, "Ulape would have laughed at me, and others would have laughed, too . . . still I would have felt the same way, for animals and birds are like people, too, though they do not talk the same or do the same things. Without them the earth would be an unhappy place." Do you agree or disagree? Explain your answer.

_____

_____

_____

_____

▮▦BEN AND ME

Read *Ben and Me: An Astonishing LIFE of BENJAMIN FRANKLIN by His Good Mouse AMOS*, discovered, edited and illustrated by Robert Lawson.

About the Author: Robert Lawson was an American author and illustrator born in 1892. He was noted for his animal stories as well as for his humorous historical stories told by the pets of famous people. Lawson incorporated historical facts with fiction, poking fun at historical people and events. In many stories, he used examples of animal society to poke fun at human society. He won the 1941 Caldecott Medal for *They Were Strong and Good* and the 1945 Newbery Medal Award for his book *Rabbit Hill*.

Discussion Topics

- What do you think about the statement made by the author in the Foreword?
- Why do you think the author claims the material was written by a mouse?
- What do you think it would be like to have a mouse ride around in your hat talking to you?
- What would your life be like if you had 25 brothers and sisters like Amos?
- What incidents from this book did you think were funny? Why?
- What is the funniest book or story you've ever read?
- For a time, elaborate wigs were the style for men, women and children. Look at the drawing of Madame Brillon's wig. What's your opinion of it?
- How would you like to wear a fancy wig every day?

Other Reading

Other books by Robert Lawson include *I Discover Columbus, Mr. Revere and I, Captain Kidd's Cat, McWhinney's Jaunt* and *Mr. Wilmer.*

Ben Franklin of Old Philadelphia by Margaret Cousins.

 AMOS

Why does Amos decide to write this book?

_____

_____

What do you think of the fur cap where Amos lived? Is
that a good place for a mouse to live? Why or why not?

_____

_____

What does Amos think of Ben's habit of going swimming?

_____

_____

What does Amos think of Ben's experiments with lightning and electricity?

_____

_____

Sometimes Amos gave useful advice. Sometimes his ideas got Ben in trouble. Give one
example from the book and explain how it caused problems for Ben.

_____

_____

Would you like to have Amos for a friend? Why or why not?

_____

_____

Amos is the oldest of the 26 children in his family. All the mice are named alphabetically. If you
were to name 26 mice from A to Z, what names would you choose? You can use real names or
made-up words to name them.

A. _____   B. _____   C. _____

D. _____   E. _____   F. _____

G. _____   H. _____   I. _____

J. _____   K. _____   L. _____

M. _____   N. _____   O. _____

P. _____   Q. _____   R. _____

S. _____   T. _____   U. _____

V. _____   W. _____   X. _____

Y. _____   Z. _____

BEN

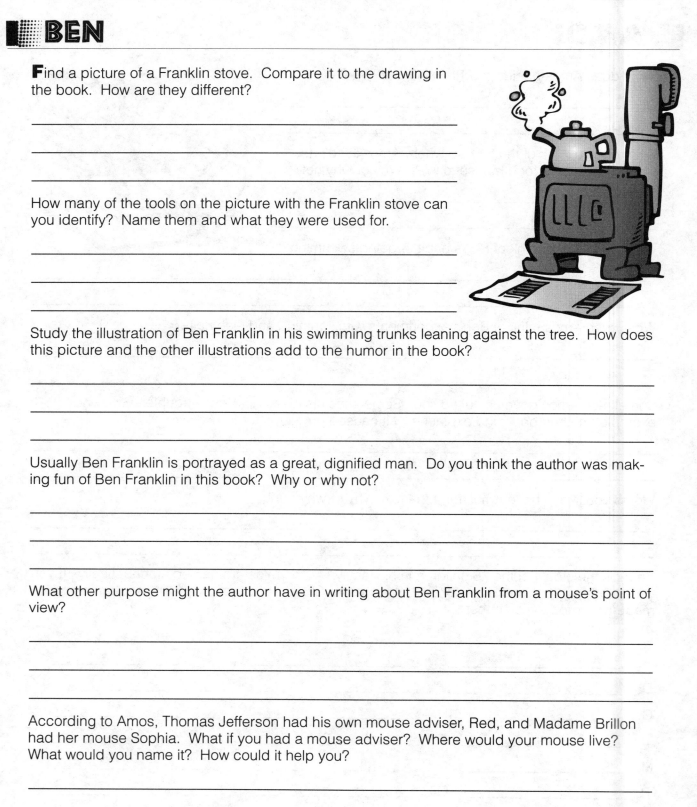

Find a picture of a Franklin stove. Compare it to the drawing in the book. How are they different?

_____

_____

_____

How many of the tools on the picture with the Franklin stove can you identify? Name them and what they were used for.

_____

_____

_____

Study the illustration of Ben Franklin in his swimming trunks leaning against the tree. How does this picture and the other illustrations add to the humor in the book?

_____

_____

_____

Usually Ben Franklin is portrayed as a great, dignified man. Do you think the author was making fun of Ben Franklin in this book? Why or why not?

_____

_____

_____

What other purpose might the author have in writing about Ben Franklin from a mouse's point of view?

_____

_____

_____

According to Amos, Thomas Jefferson had his own mouse adviser, Red, and Madame Brillon had her mouse Sophia. What if you had a mouse adviser? Where would your mouse live? What would you name it? How could it help you?

_____

_____

_____

▉ WORDS OF WISDOM

Ben Franklin is well-known for his maxims (sayings) published in *Poor Richard's Almanack*. What does Amos think of Ben's words of wisdom?

_____

_____

What do these words by Amos mean: *Maxims don't fill empty stomachs*?

_____

_____

Explain one of these sayings in your own words:

- Three may keep a secret if two are dead.
- A penny saved is a penny earned.
- Early to bed, early to rise, makes a man happy, healthy and wise.
- Fish and visitors stink in three days.
- Waste not, want not.
- The cat in gloves catches no mice.
- Forewarned is forearmed.

_____

_____

_____

Write a maxim of your own.

_____

_____

Complete one of the following activities:

- Write a short rhyming poem about a mouse who lives in a fur hat. Start by listing words that rhyme with *mouse* and *hat*.
- Study a copy of the *Farmer's Almanac*. How is it like *Poor Richard's Almanack*?
- Most homes and barns used to have lightning rods on their roofs. Why? Why don't most buildings have lightning rods today?
- How is the plot to save Sophia's children similar to events in the French Revolution?
- Write a story about Thomas Jefferson, Patrick Henry, Betsy Ross, Paul Revere, George Washington or another person from the Revolutionary War period from the point of view of their own mouse.

IN THE YEAR OF THE BOAR AND JACKIE ROBINSON

Read *In the Year of the Boar and Jackie Robinson* by Bette Bao Lord.

About the Author: Like Shirley Temple Wong, Bette Bao Lord made the long journey from China to the United States when she was only eight years old. Born in Shanghai, China, in 1938, she moved to the U.S. with her family in 1946. After receiving degrees from Tufts University and Fletcher School of Law and Diplomacy, she taught and performed modern dance for several years. She has received several awards for her children's books. *In the Year of the Boar and Jackie Robinson* was chosen as a Notable Book by the American Library Association.

Character Sketch

How do you think Mabel looked? What do you think the Señora looked like? In the box below, do an illustration or cartoon drawing of one character in the book. Next to your drawing, list at least 10 adjectives that describe that character.

Discussion Topics

- Did you like this book? Why or why not?
- Was this a sad story? Was it a humorous story? Explain your answer by giving examples.
- What was your favorite incident in the book? Why?
- Although the story is fiction, in what ways did it seem real?
- Would you like a friend like Shirley? Why or why not?
- Which character in the book, besides Shirley, would you most like for a friend? Why?
- How would you feel if your family decided to move to another country?

Other Reading

Spring Moon: A Novel of China and *Eighth Moon: The True Story of a Young Girl's Life in Communist China* by Bette Bao Lord.

WORDS TO KNOW

Write a short definition for the words listed under each chapter name.

January

abacus _____

brazier _____

celestial _____

festooned _____

matriarch _____

patriarch _____

February

dapper _____

lacquered _____

ogled _____

replica _____

rickshaw _____

March

escapade _____

flinched _____

April

gossamer _____

illustrious _____

odious _____

persuasive _____

sapphire _____

May

formidable _____

interrogate _____

intimidated _____

regale _____

June

pauper _____

ushered _____

July

dallied _____

emanated _____

mayhem _____

plague _____

sultry _____

August

alchemy _____

lolled _____

meticulous _____

talisman _____

transmuted _____

September

composure _____

warranted _____

October

phenomenon _____

November

betrothed _____

elixir _____

filial _____

jasmine _____

pomegranates _____

December

confetti _____

debut _____

feigned _____

futility _____

pessimistic _____

▌▒ INTERVIEW

An **interview** is a meeting with someone to learn more about them. Reporters and journalists conduct interviews before writing articles about people. During the interview, the reporter may ask questions about a person's entire life or about a specific incident.

Prepare a list of questions, then interview someone who . . .

A. grew up in the forties or B. immigrated to the U.S.

Examples of questions:

- How was your childhood different than mine?
- What were your favorite foods?
- How important was your family?
- What kind of clothes did your wear?
- What was your home like?
- Where did you grow up?
- What were your favorite games or sports?

List other questions you could ask during an interview.

_____

_____

Tape your interview or make notes as the person talks. List four facts you learned about the person during the interview.

1. _____

2. _____

3. _____

4. _____

List four ways that person's childhood was different than yours.

1. _____

2. _____

3. _____

4. _____

Describe the most unusual or interesting event you learned.

_____

_____

_____

■ OTHER ACTIVITIES

Complete the assigned activities.

- ■ Illustrate one scene from the story.

- ■ Explain how to determine batting averages.

- ■ Write a short report about Jackie Robinson's baseball career.

- ■ In China, Shirley lived with 32 relatives. List four advantages and four disadvantages to living with so many relatives.

- ■ In the first chapter, Shirley played a game called Pick-Up Beans. Demonstrate how you think this game might be played.

- ■ Write a report or do an illustration of how Chinese New Year is celebrated.

- ■ In the chapter "June," the teacher gave several reasons why baseball is so popular in the United States. Why do you think baseball is popular?

- ■ Jackie Robinson played for the Brooklyn Dodgers? How did this team get their name? Whatever happened to the Brooklyn Dodgers?

- ■ Shirley's friend, Mabel, made up a cheer when she was happy. Write your own cheer, and perform it with actions for the class.

- ■ Write a letter from Shirley to Fourth Cousin describing her life in Brooklyn.

- ■ Describe the Señora from Toscanini's point of view.

- ■ Imagine you were about to move to China. What are the first five things you would want or need to learn?

- ■ Write a sequel to *In the Year of the Boar and Jackie Robinson* that takes place 5, 10, 15 or 20 years later.

- ■ Bette Bao Lord uses many similes. A **simile** is a figure of speech that compares two items using the words *like* or *as*. List at least 10 examples of similes found in the book.

- ■ Learn to read and write 10 words in Chinese.

- ■ 1947 was the "Year of the Boar" in China. What does that mean? What is this year called in China?

▣ COMPARE AND CONTRAST

To **compare** means to look at ways items, events or ideas are similar. To **contrast** means to look at ways they are different.

How is your life like Shirley's? How is it different? Read the statements about Shirley and her family. Complete the sentences to compare or contrast events in your life.

Shirley moved to a new home where everything was different.

I _____

Shirley had to attend a new school where she had no friends.

I _____

Shirley made friends through baseball.

I _____

Shirley liked to help her father fix things.

I _____

Shirley chose her new name: Shirley Temple Wong. I would like to change my name to

_____ because _____

_____

Shirley enjoyed listening to the radio and reading newspapers.

I _____

Shirley's mother used a wringer washer and hung clothes on the line to dry.

We _____

Shirley took piano lessons.

I _____

Shirley liked taking care of Toscanini but had no pets of her own.

I _____

Shirley bravely offered to fix the blown fuse, even though she was scared.

I _____

TALES OF A FOURTH GRADE NOTHING

Read *Tales of a Fourth Grade Nothing* by Judy Blume.

About the Author: Judy Sussman Blume was named Elizabeth when she was born in New Jersey in 1938. As an author of books for young people, she has earned a reputation for dealing frankly with issues of interest to young readers.

The Smell of Turtle

Peter's mother says the turtle smells. Peter decides Dribble smells like turtle. Describe the smell of turtle.

_____

Describe these other smells.

Fresh baked bread:

_____

A locker room after gym class:

_____

A spring day in the country:

_____

A small pond filled with algae:

_____

Hot cocoa on a cold day:

_____

A bouquet of roses:

_____

Write a Jingle

Peter's father writes TV commercials. Write a jingle to sell a new cereal called SPLIVER. It tastes like spinach and liver.

_____

Other Reading

You can read more about the characters found in *Tales of a Fourth Grade Nothing* in *Otherwise Known as Sheila the Great*, *Superfudge* and *Fudge-A-Mania*, also by Judy Blume.

Other books by Judy Blume: *Freckle Juice; Blubber; Then Again, Maybe I Won't* and *Are You There God? It's Me, Margaret*.

▉ PETER AND FUDGE

A Telephone Message: Write a message Peter might have left on his father's answering machine after Fudge swallowed Dribble.

_____

Time to Eat: When Fudge refuses to eat, Peter suggests they leave him alone. When he got hungry enough he would eat. Peter's father had a different solution. Which idea do you think was better? Why?

_____

What would you do if your younger brother or sister refused to eat?

_____

A Fourth Grade Nothing: Sometimes Peter feels unloved. Sometimes he is jealous of Fudge. Why do you think he calls himself a fourth grade nothing?

_____

Do you think Peter is a nothing?

_____

Pet Names: Peter names his turtle Dribble. When he gets a dog, he names it Turtle. Do you think Dribble is a good name for a turtle? Is Turtle a good name for a dog?

Imagine having the following pets. What would you name each one?

A snake _____   A cat _____

A mouse _____   A dog _____

A gerbil _____   A lizard _____

A parrot _____   A monkey _____

What kind of a pet would you most like to have? _____

Why? _____

What would you name your pet? _____

WHAT WERE YOU LIKE WHEN YOU WERE THREE?

Do you think Fudge is a typical three-year-old? Why or why not?

_____

_____

Ask your parents to tell you about some strange, funny or unusual things you did when you were three. Describe or illustrate one incident below.

OTHER ACTIVITIES

Complete the assigned activities.

- Why do you think the author chose the title *Tales of a Fourth Grade Nothing* for this book? Do you think it is a good title? Why or why not?
- Select one incident when Peter feels jealous of Fudge. Describe how you would have felt if you had been Peter.
- Compare *Tales of a Fourth Grade Nothing* to another book by Judy Blume.
- Compare this book to a book by Beverly Cleary.
- Select one incident in the book. Describe something similar that happened to you and how you felt about it.
- Illustrate the funniest incident in the story.
- Make up a game or activity to keep four lively three-year-olds happy and out of trouble for half an hour at a birthday party.

Discussion Topics

- Would you like to have a brother like Fudge? Why or why not?
- If Peter were graded on being a big brother, would he get an A, B, C, D or F? Why?
- Why do some people prefer nicknames to their real names? Why did Farley prefer to be called Fudge? Why didn't Peter's mother want him to call his brother Fang? Why would parents name a child Farley?
- In the beginning of the book, Mr. and Mrs. Yarby make remarks about children and manners. Do you think it was Peter and Fudge who lacked manners or Mr. and Mrs. Yarby?
- Do you think Peter's parents expected him to help out too much with Fudge? Why or why not?
- What did you think was the funniest part of the story? Why?
- Why didn't Peter want another turtle after Fudge swallowed Dribble?
- Why were Peter's parents upset when Fudge swallowed the turtle? Why was Peter upset?
- Is this story about Peter or Fudge? Who is the main character?
- If you have younger brothers or sisters, how are they like Fudge? How are they different?
- What pets do you have? How did your pets get their names?

SARAH, PLAIN AND TALL

Read *Sarah, Plain and Tall* by Patricia MacLachlan. Can you visualize Sarah, Anna, Caleb and their father?

About the Author: Patricia MacLachlan was born in Cheyenne, Wyoming. After graduating from the University of Connecticut, she became an English teacher and lecturer on children's literature. She has written picture books and novels for children. *Sarah, Plain and Tall* won the 1986 Newbery Medal Award.

Discussion Topics

- What is the mood at the beginning of the book?
- What is the mood at the end of the book?
- If you had been Anna and Caleb, how would you have felt if your father put an ad in the paper for a wife?
- What do you think the term *mail order bride* means?
- Some people sing when they are happy. Some sing when they are sad. When do you sing? What songs do you like to sing?
- Why doesn't papa sing anymore?
- Why is singing so important to Caleb?
- What does *ayuh* mean?
- Why does Papa say he will answer "ayuh" when the preacher asks him if he will marry Sarah?
- Maggie was also a "mail order bride." She understood how Sarah felt. "There are always things to miss," said Maggie. "No matter where you are." What did she mean?

Your Picture of Sarah

How do you picture Sarah? Is she riding in the wagon wearing a blue dress and a yellow bonnet? Is she wearing overalls and fixing the roof? Is she swimming in the cow pond in her petticoat? Draw a picture of Sarah the way you think she looked.

Other Reading

Other books by Patricia MacLachlan include *Unclaimed Treasures*; *Cassie Binegar*; *Arthur, for the Very First Time*; *The Facts and Fictions of Minna Pratt*; *Seven Kisses in a Row* and *Tomorrow's Wizard*.

◼▦ SARAH

Why do you think Sarah answered the ad?

_____

_____

What do you learn about Sarah from her letters?

_____

_____

_____

If you had been Anna and Caleb, would you have been eager to meet Sarah? Why or why not?

_____

Why were Anna and Caleb eager to meet Sarah?

_____

Why do you think Sarah made the long, difficult journey from Maine to meet Jacob, Anna and Caleb?

_____

_____

Do you think Sarah planned to stay when she first arrived? Why or why not?

_____

What clues show that Sarah likes the children and Papa and her new home?

_____

What clues show she misses her home in Maine?

_____

"Sarah is Sarah. She does things her way, you know." What does Papa mean by that?

_____

What does Sarah miss about her home?

_____

Sarah says she will always miss her old home, but she would miss them more if she left. Why?

_____

TLC10032 Copyright © Teaching & Learning Company, Carthage, IL 62321

ANNA AND CALEB

How old do you think Anna and Caleb are? Give reasons for your answer.

_____

_____

What questions would you have asked Sarah in a letter if you had been Anna?

_____

_____

What questions would you have asked Sarah in a letter if you had been Caleb?

_____

_____

In Chapter 3, Anna and Caleb wait for their father to return with Sarah.   The author repeats words and phrases like . . . Maybe, maybe . . . a woodchuck ate and listened. Ate and listened. Caleb rolled a marble back and forth. Back and forth. What does this repetition of words tell us about how Anna and Caleb felt then?

_____

Do you think Sarah was what they expected? Explain your answer.

_____

_____

Why did the children fear Sarah wouldn't stay?

_____

_____

What are Caleb's ideas for keeping Sarah from leaving?

_____

_____

When Sarah returned from town, Caleb burst into tears and cried, "Seal was very worried." What did he really mean?

_____

_____

_____

_____

_____

DECISIONS, DECISIONS

Why do you think Papa decided to put an ad in a newspaper for a wife?

_____

_____

Do you think it was an easy decision? Why or why not?

_____

_____

Why didn't he tell his children about the ad until after he received a reply?

_____

_____

The neighbors brought Sarah three chickens and some plants for her garden. Why were these good gifts? How did these gifts help Sarah decide to stay?

_____

_____

Why do you think Sarah decided to stay?

_____

_____

Do you think it was an easy decision for her? Why or why not?

_____

_____

The children and Papa were worried that Sarah would leave, but they did not ask her if she was going to stay. They wanted to know why she wanted to go to town alone. Why do you think they didn't ask her these questions?

_____

_____

When you have to make a difficult decision, what do you do?

_____

_____

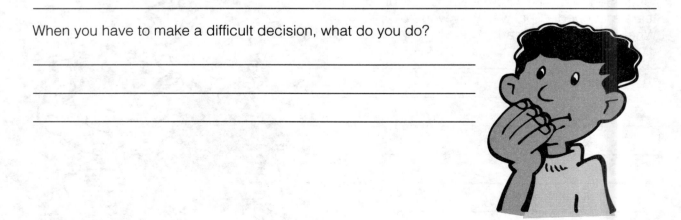

THE TWENTY-ONE BALLOONS

Read *The Twenty-One Balloons* by William Péne du Bois.

About the Author: William Péne du Bois was born in 1916 in Nutley, New Jersey. Not only is he a noted writer, he has also illustrated more than 50 books, winning the prestigious Caldecott Award twice. At the age of eight, he moved to France with his family and attended school there until they moved back to the U.S. when he was 14. He published his first book when he was only 19. William Péne du Bois is best known for combining adventure, fantasy and humor in his stories.

The Twenty-One Balloons, winner of the 1948 Newbery Medal Award, is the story of an incredible balloon voyage made in 1883. As the author says in the introduction, "Half of this story is true and the other half might very well have happened."

Other Reading

Other books by William Péne du Bois include *The Great Geppy, Peter Graves, The Giant, Lion, The Alligator Case, Gentleman Bear, Lazy Tommy Pumpkinhead, Otto at Sea, Otto in Texas* and *Otto in Africa*.

Chapter by Chapter

Introduction

Read *The Twenty-One Balloons* by William Péne du Bois. Complete the activities below when you finish the Introduction.

What does the word *conveyance* mean?

_____

Which of the two ways to travel described in the introduction do you prefer? Why?

_____

_____

Would you like to travel in the manner the author predicts for the future—by walking through a door from one continent to another? Why or why not?

_____

_____

What would be the first place you'd visit if you could walk through a door to anywhere on Earth? Why?

_____

_____

Why would a balloon be a good way to travel to school?

_____

CHAPTER BY CHAPTER

Chapters I and II

Define the words listed before you read the chapters. Complete
the activities when you finish reading Chapters I and II.

Chapter I. Professor Sherman's Incredible Loyalty

singular _____

illustrious _____

fraternity _____

ascension _____

deflate _____

flotsam _____

unprecedented _____

If you were a reporter, what three questions would you most like the professor to answer?

1. _____

2. _____

3. _____

Chapter II. A Hero's Welcome Is Prepared

surmounted _____

brace _____

dirigible _____

cupola _____

decisively _____

motif _____

What did the people of San Francisco do to welcome Professor Sherman?

_____

What do you think might have happened to the 58-pound boy if he hadn't been able to grab on
to the church spire?

_____

Would you like to travel on a sofa held up by balloons and pulled by horses? Why or why not?

_____

CHAPTER BY CHAPTER

Chapters III and IV

Define the words listed before you read the chapters. Complete the activities when you finish reading Chapters III and IV.

Chapter III. A Description of the *Globe*

lackey _____

waif _____

tumultuous _____

ballast _____

Professor Sherman says the ambition of explorers was to go where no one had gone before. Do you agree or disagree? Why?

_____

Would you like to live alone in a balloon house for a year? Why or why not?

_____

What would you pack for a long balloon trip?

_____

Why are balsa wood, bamboo and wicker good materials to use for a balloon house?

_____

What is your opinion of Professor Sherman's method for washing clothes and dishes?

_____

_____

Chapter IV. The Unwelcome Passenger

altitude _____

balustrade _____

catastrophic _____

rarefied _____

What caused the Professor's balloon to deflate?

_____

What did the Professor hope to accomplish by throwing everything overboard after the balloon began to descend?

_____

_____

_____

CHAPTER BY CHAPTER

Chapter V

Define the words listed before you read the chapter. Complete the activities when you finish reading Chapter V.

Chapter V. A New Citizen of Krakatoa

delirious _____

aristocrat _____

desolate _____

ascot _____

absurd _____

". . . being on Krakatoa was like riding on the back of some giant prehistoric animal." Explain what Professor Sherman meant.

_____

What are "mountain legs"?

_____

Why did Mr. F. tell the professor that he would have to live on Krakatoa for the rest of his life?

_____

"That's the particular thing about nature," explained Mr. F., "it guards its rarest treasures with greatest care." What did Mr. F. mean?

_____

Where is Krakatoa?

_____

Krakatoa is located in the Sunda Strait, south of Sumatra and west of Java, Indonesia. Find this area on the map and draw in the Island of Krakatoa.

CHAPTER BY CHAPTER

Chapter VI

Define the words listed before you read the chapter. Complete the activities when you finish reading Chapter VI.

Chapter VI. The Gourmet Government

gourmet _____

antique _____

canopied (bed) _____

exquisite _____

fleur-de-lis _____

opulence _____

Would you like a bedroom like the one Professor Sherman slept in on Krakatoa? Why or why not?

_____

The ground "looked like animated furrows in a plowed field," said the professor. What did he mean?

_____

If you had been the first sailor shipwrecked on Krakatoa, what would you have done after you discovered the diamonds and built a raft?

_____

What were some of the problems the inhabitants of Krakatoa experienced at first?

_____

What is your opinion of the restaurant system of government?

_____

Why did the citizens of Krakatoa divide the months into 20 days?

_____

Why would Mr. U. be a bad name to have?

_____

CHAPTER BY CHAPTER

Chapters VII and VIII

Define the words listed before reading the chapters. Complete the activities when you finish reading Chapters VII and VIII.

Chapter VII. The Moroccan House of Marvels

hydraulic _____

minaret _____

bureau _____

intermission _____

What feature of the Moroccan House of Marvels would you most like to have in your home? Why?

_____

_____

Professor Sherman says that ". . . mechanical progress always seems to leave the slower demands of elegance far behind." What does he mean?

_____

_____

Chapter VIII. Airy-Go-Round

valet _____

trepidation _____

tarpaulin _____

Why didn't the professor admit he was a school teacher?

_____

Would you like to take a ride in an "airy-go-round"? Why or why not?

_____

What would have been the best part about being a child on Krakatoa?

_____

◼ CHAPTER BY CHAPTER

Chapters IX and X

Define the words listed before reading the chapters. Complete the activities when you finish reading Chapters IX and X.

Chapter IX. Concerning the Giant Balloon Life Raft

timidity _____

apprehension _____

nitroglycerin _____

The professor wonders why the people of Krakatoa continued to live on an island with an active volcano when they could live anywhere in the world? ". . . we have locked ourselves in a diamond prison," answers Mr. F. What does he mean?

_____

People all over the world live on volcanic islands, in areas where earthquakes occur or in places prone to terrible floods. Even after disasters, most people return and rebuild. Why?

_____

_____

Chapter X. What Goes Up Must Come Down

hospitality _____

curry _____

doddered _____

floundered _____

catapulted _____

concussion _____

Although the emergency plan to leave the island has been well-rehearsed and carefully planned, it does not go as smoothly as expected. Why?

_____

What was the most believable part of this story?

_____

_____

What was the most unbelievable part of this story?

_____

_____

On a globe, trace Professor Sherman's route from San Francisco to Krakatoa across India, Europe and the Atlantic Ocean.

▉ THE TROUBLE WITH TUCK

Read *The Trouble with Tuck* by Theodore Taylor. As you read, think about what you would have done if you had been Helen.

About the Author: Born in 1922, Theodore Taylor began working as a reporter when he was only 13. He joined the *Washington Daily News* at the age of 17 and became an NBC sportswriter by the time he was 19. Over the years, Theodore Taylor held many different jobs including merchant sailor, naval officer, magazine writer, movie publicist and documentary film-maker. He has written books for both adults and children.

The Trouble with Tuck was published in 1981. The events in the story took place in the mid 1950s and are based on a true story.

Discussion Topics

- Who is telling the story? Would the story be different if it were told from Helen's mother's or father's point of view?
- What if the story were told from Tuck's or Lady Daisy's point of view?
- Do you think animals can be happy or unhappy? Why or why not?
- What is self-confidence?
- What examples show Helen lacked self-confidence at the beginning of the book?
- What incidents show how Helen is gaining self-confidence throughout the story?
- How can students your age get more self-confidence?
- Do you think a pet can help a person become more self-confident? Why or why not?
- Give some examples from the book that show how Helen and her family were devoted to Tuck.
- If you had been Helen, would you have worked as hard to help Tuck? Why or why not?

Other Reading

Other books by Theodore Taylor include *Teetoncey, The Cay, The Maldonado Miracle, The Children's War, Teetoncey and Ben O'Neal, The Odyssey of Ben O'Neal, Battle in the Arctic Sea* and *The Hostage.*

▌ WHAT DO YOU THINK?

Helen says her mother, ". . . was always one to keep things in order." How was that also true of Helen?

_____

How would you feel if you were carrying a birthday cake, tripped and fell face first into the cake?

_____

Have you ever had something embarrassing like that happen to you? You don't have to tell what happened unless you want to. Describe how you felt when it happened.

_____

When she made the appointment at the California Companion Dogs for the Blind, why didn't Helen tell the woman that the "someone" in the family who was blind was a dog?

_____

Why do you think Mrs. Chaffey changed her mind about a seeing eye dog for Tuck?

_____

Although she had not succeeded in training Tuck and Lady Daisy, in Chapter 15, Helen's parents tell her they are proud of her for trying so hard. Helen says, "Those words or words like them, have been said to daughters and sons since the cave days, I suspect, but they don't take you off the hook of failure." What does Helen mean?

_____

_____

_____

At the end of the book, Helen marches with the dogs down the street whistling the "Colonel Bogey" march from the movie *The Bridge on the River Kwai*. Listen to a recording of this song.

Why was it appropriate for Helen to whistle this song?

_____

_____

_____

◼ ABOUT HELEN

Helen said, "I had no self-confidence and that's why I whistled." Name some other habits people have that show when they are nervous.

_____

_____

Why do you think people have these kinds of habits?

_____

"Looking back, I see it was the start of a 'new' me," Helen says at the end of Chapter 3. What does she mean?

_____

When she hits her head on the diving board, Helen says ". . . I had proved once again that if there was a way to mess things up, I'd find it." Why did Helen say that?

_____

When Helen decided to run away, she says, "Not once did I think about doing anything wrong. My goal was to take Tuck away from danger and nothing else mattered." What danger did Helen think Tuck was in?

_____

How did she think running away with him would help?

_____

At first, what did Helen's family think of the idea of a seeing eye dog for Tuck?

_____

_____

What did they think of the idea after Helen started training Lady Daisy?

_____

When her parents and Mrs. Chaffey decide to give up on the training, Helen persists. Why?

_____

How did Helen finally accomplish the training?

_____

_____

_____

ABOUT TUCK

When Helen received the tiny puppy she knew ". . . it was very important that he have the exact right name. A 'Rover' or a human name like 'Jack' would not do." Why was it important for her to find the right name?

_____

How did Tuck get his name? What was his whole name?

_____

Helen called Tuck ". . . my security in the darkness, my knight of the night." How can a pet make a person feel more secure?

_____

When Tuck ran through the screen door at the beginning of the book and later when he chewed up the door in Chapter 12, Helen's parents didn't get angry. Why not?

_____

How were Helen's family willing to help her and Tuck?

_____

How did Tuck help Helen become more self-confident?

_____

Her father told Helen not to feel sorry for Tuck when he wouldn't cooperate with her. How did feeling sorry for Tuck make it more difficult for Helen to train him?

_____

Select one of the three options below. From Tuck's point of view, write a paragraph about . . .

    A. What it was like to be a blind dog

    B. What it was like to be chained up

    C. What it was like during the training with Lady Daisy

_____

_____

_____

_____

_____

_____

PERSONAL CLOUDS

"**M**other always worked around her flowers when she was upset, claiming the feel of the damp earth helped chase personal clouds away."

Personal clouds could be people or events that upset you, like visiting a relative you don't like or going to the dentist.

Write some of your "personal clouds" below.

What do you do to chase away your "personal clouds"?

_____

Self-Confidence Is . . .

- ■ Self-confidence is singing a solo in front of the whole school.
- ■ Self-confidence is flying on an airplane all alone.

What do you think self-confidence is? Complete the lines below.

Self-confidence is _____

Self-confidence is _____

Self-confidence is _____

WHO STOLE THE WIZARD OF OZ?

Read *Who Stole The Wizard of Oz?* by Avi. As you read, follow the clues to see if you can figure out "whodunit" and why before you get to the end of the story.

Discussion Topics

- How would you like to have a teacher like Miss McPhearson?

- In *Who Stole The Wizard of Oz?* there are two mysteries to solve. What are they?

- Why was Becky so persistent in trying to find who stole the library books?

- Toby claims the best way to read a book is by flashlight under the covers in bed. Where do you like to read?

- ". . . one of the best things about Gramp is that you can ask him anything, and he'll give you an answer—but he won't try to find out why you're asking." Why would Toby think that was important?

- After reading *Winnie-the-Pooh*, Becky says that she knows two Eyeores and five Piglets. Describe people who are like Eyeore and people who are like Piglet.

- From what you learned about Miss Tobias, do you think you would have liked her? Why or why not?

- A clue that leads you in the wrong direction is called a "red herring." What are some red herrings in this story?

Other Reading

The Sherlock Holmes Mysteries by Arthur Conan Doyle.

From the Mixed-Up Files of Mrs. Basil E. Frankweiler by E.L. Konigsburg.

Einstein Anderson, Science Sleuth and other books about Einstein Anderson by Seymor Simon.

Encyclopedia Brown, Boy Detective and other books about Encyclopedia Brown by Donald J. Sobol.

▛ WHODUNIT?

Why do you think mysteries are sometimes called "whodunits"?

List three possible suspects that might have stolen *The Wizard of Oz?* and the other books from the library. List reasons why each was a suspect.

1. _____

2. _____

3. _____

List places the treasure might have been hidden and why.

_____

_____

Before you finished reading the story, who did you think stole the books from the library? Why?

_____

Miss McPhearson

"No mysteries, no make-believe, no romantic adventures . . . Children your age are beyond such nonsense. This list contains nothing but basic, useful information," Miss McPhearson told her class.

List five books that Miss McPhearson would consider useful.

1. _____

2. _____

3. _____

4. _____

5. _____

List five books that Miss McPhearson would not consider useful.

1. _____

2. _____

3. _____

4. _____

5. _____

How can mysteries, romantic adventures and make-believe be informative?

_____

▮ YOUR OWN MYSTERY

Work with a small group to write and solve your own mystery story.

The mystery: Your school basketball team is scheduled to play the final championship game next Saturday against Central. On Monday morning, the Coach discovered that someone stole all the basketballs from the school gym.

Clues

- Josh says he hates basketball. The Coach cut him from the team last Friday for cheating on a test.
- Two members of the Central team were seen on the school playground on Sunday morning.
- The custodian saw someone who looked like the substitute teacher, Mr. Hanney in the gym early Monday morning before school started. Mr. Hanney used to teach at Central.
- The Coach left the keys to the gym in his unlocked car over the weekend. Sara lives next door to the Coach.

Make up three more clues about the missing basketballs.

1. _____
2. _____
3. _____

List four reasons why the basketballs might have been stolen.

1. _____
2. _____
3. _____
4. _____

List three possible suspects and reasons why they might have taken the basketballs.

1. _____
2. _____
3. _____

Solve the case. Who stole the basketballs and why? How did you figure it out?

ESCAPE TO WITCH MOUNTAIN

Read *Escape to Witch Mountain* by Alexander Key. As you read, notice how Tia's memories help to fill in the background for the story.

About the Author: Alexander Key was born in La Plata, Maryland, in 1904. He lost both parents as a child and grew up living with various relatives. He began his career as a book illustrator, completing his first book at the age of 19 while still a student at the Chicago Art Institute. He later taught art in Chicago at the Studio School of Art. Alexander Key began writing children's books and stories in 1929 and later wrote adult fiction and magazine articles. His book, *Escape to Witch Mountain* was made into a Disney movie.

Discussion Topics

- The author portrays most authority figures as being either unkind, greedy or evil. Give examples from the story.
- What people do not understand, they fear or hate. Why?
- "Does everything have to make sense? People would say that we didn't make sense, just because we're not like everybody else." Why is it difficult for people to accept others who are different?
- Why were people so ready to believe the children were witches?
- Why is Castaway an appropriate name for those who came to Earth?
- Why did Tony feel they should not join the other Castaways when they appeared to be so close to safety at the end?
- Why did the other Castaways want Tia and Tony to be seen picked up by the spaceship?
- Tony explains that when his people arrived on Earth, they didn't understand the idea of individual land ownership or the importance of money. To his people, actually living and doing were the important things in life. What did Tony mean by "living and doing"?
- Do you think Father O'Day was one of the Castaways? Why or why not?
- Did you like this book? Why or why not?

Other Reading

Other books by Alexander Key include *The Forgotten Door*, *The Golden Enemy* and *The Incredible Tide*.

MRS. GRINDLEY AND HACKETT HOUSE

"**F**rom the expressionless way Mrs. Grindley looked them over—as if she were viewing a pair of strange and doubtful fish that had been dredged up from the harbor depths—Tony knew that the days ahead were not going to be overflowing with sweetness and light." Is his prediction correct? Give an example from the book.

_____

_____

What do you think it would have been like to live at Hackett House?

_____

_____

Mrs. Grindley doesn't like Tia and Tony. Do you think it has anything to do with them personally, or is that the way she feels about most people?

_____

_____

Do you think Mrs. Grindley likes children? Why is she in charge of a children's home?

_____

_____

When Lucas Deranian shows up and claims he is their uncle, Tia and Tony do not want to go with him. Mrs. Grindley tells them, "You ought to be thankful you have someone who's willing to look after you. Don't you want to live in a decent home—or don't you even realize how lucky you are?" Why is she so willing to let him take them away even though they object?

_____

_____

Mrs. Grindley tells the children, "I'm sure the court isn't going to turn you over to him unless he's able to prove he's all right, and that he can give you a good home." Do you think she really believes that? If not, why does she say it?

_____

_____

◼ TIA AND TONY

Tia says, "If there are more people as different as we are, then well—maybe we're members of a different race of people." How are Tia and Tony unlike other people?

_____

What special talents did they have?

_____

Why did they take care to hide their talents from other people?

_____

If you could have any one of the talents Tia or Tony had, which one would you choose? Why?

_____

Although Tony is older, he often defers to his sister. "Tia could feel things he couldn't, and he'd learned it always paid to follow her instincts." Give an example where it paid to follow Tia's instincts.

_____

How did the harmonica make Tony stronger?

_____

"Somehow he had to get it (the harmonica) back, for he might need it later in an emergency." How did the harmonica help Tony later in an emergency?

_____

_____

How do Tia's returning memories fill in gaps in the story?

_____

_____

What do you think Tia and Tony's life was like after they joined the Castaways?

_____

_____

▊ WHAT DO YOU THINK?

Why do you think Lucas Deranian wanted to find the children so badly?

_____

_____

Who do you think he was working for?

_____

_____

What do you think would have happened to Tia and Tony if he had gotten custody of them?

_____

_____

Why do you think Father O'Day believed the children?

_____

_____

Would you have believed their story if they had come to you for help?

_____

_____

Tia tells Tony that Winkie is "not any ordinary cat, anymore than we are ordinary people." What do you think is different about Winkie?

_____

_____

"It's simple enough, Tony. If you have any real feeling for animals, you'd know exactly how they feel, and that's practically the same as being able to talk to them," Tia says. What do you think she means?

_____

_____

At the end of the book: "After all that had happened, he knew it would be much wiser to wait a while before he joined the children on Witch Mountain." Why would Father O'Day want to join the people on Witch Mountain?

_____

_____

Do you think the people on Witch Mountain would welcome Father O'Day? Why or why not?

_____

THE UGLY DUCKLING

Read "The Ugly Duckling" by Hans Christian Andersen.

About the Author: Born in Denmark in 1805, Hans Christian Andersen left home at the age of 14. He worked as an actor in Copenhagen for a time before attending Copenhagen University. His first four fairy tales were published in 1835 in *Tales Told for Children*.

Hans Christian Andersen published poetry, novels, plays, travel sketches and memoirs, but he is best remembered as the creator of fairy tales for children. His 168 stories, which combine fantasy and wisdom, have been published in more than 100 languages.

Discussion Topics

- How would you have felt if you were the mother duck and hatched an "ugly" duckling?
- How would you have felt if you were the ugly duckling?
- Like the ducks in the barnyard, people have trouble accepting those who are different. Why?
- How is this story like a fable?
- How is the mother duck's view of the ugly duckling different than the other animals? How is it similar?
- Did you like this story? Why or why not?
- What lessons can people learn from "The Ugly Duckling"?
- How do you think the mother duck felt after the ugly duckling ran away? Explain your answer.
- Hans Christian Andersen's stories have been published in more than 100 languages. Why do you think they have such universal appeal?

Other Reading

"The Steadfast Tin Soldier," "The Tinderbox," "The Princess and the Pea," "The Emperor's New Clothes," "The Snow Queen," "The Little Match Girl," "The Red Shoes" and "The Little Fir Tree" are other stories by Hans Christian Andersen.

ACTIVITIES

Complete the assigned activities after you read "The Ugly Duckling" by Hans Christian Andersen.

■ How does this saying apply to the story of the ugly duckling? "Things are not always what they seem."

■ Compare "The Ugly Duckling" to another story by Hans Christian Andersen.

■ Compare "The Ugly Duckling" to one of Aesop's fables. What would be the moral for this story?

■ Learn more about ducks and swans. Compare and contrast the two types of birds.

■ After the first winter, the ugly duckling sees three swans. He approaches them, even though he fears they will kill him. He felt it was better to be killed by them than to be snapped at by the ducks, pecked by the hens or suffer another miserable winter. Why?

■ At the end of the story, when the ugly duckling realizes he is a swan, why was he "glad of all the misery and tribulation he had gone through"?

■ What do you think this sentence means? "He was very happy, but not at all proud, for a good heart never becomes proud."

■ Illustrate this story using at least four drawings showing the events in the story.

■ Invent an interpretive dance to tell the story without words. Use any type of music for background that you think is appropriate.

■ Animals are the main characters in "The Ugly Duckling," but the story could apply as well to people. How?

■ Many of Andersen's stories reveal a deep, pessimistic insight into human nature. How does this apply to "The Ugly Duckling"?

■ Learn more about the life of Hans Christian Andersen.

■ Write a short poem based on the story.

■ Rewrite the story as if it were a newspaper article. Be sure to answer the questions who, what, when, where, why and how in the lead paragraph.

HAIL AND FAREWELL

Read "Hail and Farewell" by Ray Bradbury found in the short story collection *S Is for Space*.

About the Author: Ray Bradbury was born in Waukegan, Illinois, in 1920. His formal education ended when he graduated from high school in Los Angeles in 1938. Bradbury's first story was published in 1941. Sometimes called a science fiction writer, sometimes known as a writer of fantasy, he has published hundreds of short stories, stage and screenplays, novels and articles. Over the years Bradbury has received many awards for his writing including the O'Henry Memorial Award, The Benjamin Franklin Award and the Aviation-Space Writer's award.

Discussion Topics

■ How is Willie different from other boys?

■ What was Willie's "job"?

■ What advantages would someone have who stayed 12 years old forever?

■ What disadvantages would someone have who never grew up?

■ Do you think Willie would have chosen to grow up if he could?

■ Would you like to stay 12 forever? Why or why not?

■ What did the people who adopted Willie gain from him?

■ What did Willie gain from the people who adopted him?

■ Compare "Hail and Farewell" to the story of Peter Pan.

■ Do you think Willie was lonely? Why or why not?

■ What kind of people did Willie look for to adopt him? Why?

■ Ray Bradbury is often classified as a science fiction writer. Would you call this a science fiction story? Why or why not?

Other Reading

Other books by Ray Bradbury include *The Martian Chronicles, The Golden Apples of the Sun, The Illustrated Man, Timeless Stories for Today and Tomorrow, Dandelion Wine, Something Wicked This Way Comes, Fahrenheit 451, I Sing the Body Electric* and *A Medicine for Melancholy*.

◼️ WHAT DO YOU THINK?

Explain the first sentence in the story "Hail and Farewell."

"Better to've had a son thirty-six months than none whatever." What do you think this quote from the story means? Do you agree?

If you could be the same age for the rest of your life, what age would it be? Why?

Although his body never grew up, do you think Willie grew up in his mind? Why or why not?

Do you think Willie was dishonest to pretend to be a boy when he was really a man?

What other choice did Willie have other than to live the way he did?

Do you think Willie was happy? Why or why not?

Willie didn't tell his secret to the couples who adopted him until they began to guess. "Telling them would have spoiled everything." Why?

How do you think Willie's "mothers and fathers" felt after he left?

AESOP'S FABLES

A fable is a story told to teach a lesson. The lesson, which appears at the end of the fable, is called the **moral**. In most of Aesop's fables, the characters are animals who act like people.

No one knows if all the stories called Aesop's Fables were really written by one man. According to Herodotus, a fifth century Greek historian, Aesop was a Greek slave who lived in the sixth century B.C. It's likely that the stories were collected from many sources and written down over several hundred years. These fables have been written, revised and translated into many languages. Whether they were written by Aesop, or someone else, these stories have met the test of time in their appeal to young and old around the world.

Because Aesop's Fables have been rewritten so many times by so many writers, you will find many versions of the same story and sometimes different morals for the same story.

Animals as Characters

Some animals, like wolves, foxes, sheep and mice appear over and over again in Aesop's Fables. Sheep might remind people of an animal that is shy and not very intelligent. People often think of a wolf as being sly, cunning, evil, bold, treacherous, strong and smart.

After the name of each animal below, write at least three words that animal makes you think of.

Crow _____

Rabbit _____

Mouse _____

Crane _____

Stork _____

Fox _____

Eagle _____

Pig _____

Elephant _____

Cat _____

Tiger _____

Lion _____

Frog _____

Dog _____

Turtle (tortoise) _____

■ BELLING THE CAT

Read the fable "Belling the Cat." In your own words, what is the moral of the story?

_____

_____

Compare this moral to the moral in another version of the same fable. You can do this by reading more than one version of the story or by working with a partner who has read a different version.

List the two morals you found for this fable.

_____

_____

_____

How are the morals alike?

_____

_____

How are they different?

_____

_____

_____

Which moral do you think fits the story better? Why?

_____

_____

_____

Was the idea of a bell on the cat a good one? Why or why not?

_____

_____

Do you think the mice gave up too easily on the idea? Explain your answer.

_____

_____

What if the mice had given the cat a fancy silver bell for a present? If the cat wore it because she thought it was so beautiful, the mice would know when she was about. Then the story would have a different ending and a different moral. What would the moral to this story be?

_____

_____

MERCURY AND THE WOODSMAN

Read the fable "Mercury and the Woodsman." In your own words, what is the moral of this story?

_____

_____

Why do you think Mercury gave the woodsman all three axes?

_____

If you had been the woodsman, what would you have done when Mercury asked you if the gold ax was yours?

_____

What do you think would have happened if the woodsman had claimed the gold or silver ax?

_____

Give an example from your life where "honesty is the best policy" proved to be true.

_____

_____

Complete one of the following activities:

- This fable uses people rather than animals. Rewrite the fable using animals.
- Illustrate three scenes from this fable.
- Write a poem that reflects the moral of the story.
- Present a puppet show of this story to the class.
- Make up a song the woodsman might have sung on his way home with the three axes.
- Find a newspaper or magazine article that shows honesty is the best policy.
- Make an honesty collage.
- Design a costume for Mercury.
- Read a story about Mercury from mythology. Summarize the story.

THE FOX AND THE STORK

Read the fable "The Fox and the Stork" Write the moral in your own words.

_____

_____

What was the joke the fox played on the stork? _____

_____

_____

Why did the fox think it was a good joke? _____

_____

_____

How did the stork turn the tables on the fox? _____

_____

_____

Did the fox think it was a good joke when he couldn't get anything to eat? Why or why not?

_____

_____

How would you feel if someone invited you to dinner and served only food they knew you didn't like?

_____

_____

Put a check by the moral that you think best fits the fable of the fox and the stork.

_____ It's better to eat a little with friends than to feast with enemies.

_____ Turnabout is fair play.

_____ Honesty is the best policy.

_____ Don't complain when others treat you as you treat them.

_____ The best way to get something done is to do it yourself.

_____ Don't dish it out, if you can't take it.

_____ Don't be greedy.

Explain why you chose that moral.

⬛ THE TORTOISE AND THE HARE

Read the fable "The Tortoise and the Hare." In your own words, what is the moral of this story?

_____

_____

Why do you think the tortoise challenged the hare to a race?

_____

How did the tortoise win the race?

_____

How do you think the hare felt when the tortoise won?

_____

Are you more like the hare or the tortoise? Explain your answer.

_____

_____

_____

Complete one of the following activities:

- Make up a board game based on this fable.
- Rewrite this fable so the rabbit wins.
- Compare this fable to another Aesop's Fable.
- Use references to compare a tortoise to a turtle.
- Use references to compare a rabbit to a hare.
- Rewrite the story in first person from the hare's point of view.
- Rewrite the story in first person from the tortoise's point of view.
- Write a sequel to this fable to answer the question: What happened when the tortoise and the hare had a rematch?
- Present the story of the tortoise and the hare in a four-panel cartoon format.

MORE AESOP'S FABLES

Select one of the fables listed below.

- The Wind and the Sun
- The Old Man, His Son and the Donkey
- The Boy Who Cried Wolf
- The Ants and the Grasshopper
- The Town Mouse and the Country Mouse
- The Dog and His Shadow
- The Fox and the Grapes
- The Goose That Laid the Golden Egg
- The Lion and the Mouse
- The Frogs Asking for a King

Read the fable. Then complete three of the activities listed.

- Rewrite the fable in a modern setting.
- Write a song based on the fable.
- Write a nonrhyming poem based on the fable.
- Write a limerick based on the fable.
- Do an illustration of the fable.
- Write five other morals for the same fable.
- Write five other titles for the same fable.
- Present a play or puppet show based on the fable.
- Tell the fable in pantomime (without using any words).
- Rewrite the fable from the point of view of one of the characters.
- Make a collage or mosaic design based on the fable.
- Rewrite the fable as though it were a newspaper article.
- Write a TV ad based on the fable.
- If you were going to make a movie based on this fable, which actors or actresses would you select for each part? Explain your choices.
- Invent a new product based on the fable. Explain what it does, how it tastes or how it works.
- Name all the characters in the fable. Explain why you chose each name.
- Design a car, airplane, ship or other vehicle based on the fable.
- Compare this fable to another short story you've read.
- Write a 10-question test for this fable. Include an answer key.
- Write a sequel to the fable.
- Draw a four-panel cartoon based on the fable.

▘ PANDORA'S BOX

Read two versions of *Pandora's Box.*

Pandora's Box, retold and illustrated by Lisl Weil, is one of many versions of this ancient Greek myth. Another version was written by Nathaniel Hawthorne. Although the basic story and the ending are much the same, there are many differences between these two versions.

People have always wondered about things they could not understand. They looked for answers. A **myth** is a story that tries to explain nature and the world around us. Stories that explain how people were created, why the sun rises and sets every day and why we have winter are myths.

Because ancient Greece was an important political unit for about 2,000 years, many of the ideas, beliefs and stories were written down and preserved. The Greek gods and goddesses, the mortal heroes and heroines and the stories about what they did are remembered even today.

- After reading *Pandora's Box*, write a moral for this myth in your own words.
- A myth tries to explain something about the world around us. What does this myth try to explain?
- According to the story, what was the world like before Pandora opened the box? How did it change?
- Read two versions of this story. Compare how the two stories are alike and ways they are different.

Discussion Topics

- Do you think the story means people shouldn't be curious? Why or why not?
- If you had been Pandora, would you have looked in the box? Why or why not?
- If someone had told Pandora what was in the box, do you think she would have looked anyway, just to be sure?
- How does Hope help people deal with their Troubles?

▟ TROUBLE WITH A CAPITAL *T*

When Pandora opened the box, Troubles escaped into the world. There were big Troubles like war and famine, and small Troubles like chicken pox, frizzy hair and hangnails.

Work with a partner to list Troubles that might have come from Pandora's box.

_____   _____

_____   _____

_____   _____

What do you think the Troubles Pandora let loose looked like? Draw and label some Troubles coming out of the box below.

Other Reading

D'Aulaire's Book of Greek Myths by Ingri and Edgar P. D'Aulaire.

Lord of the Sky: Zeus by Doris Gates.

BAUCIS AND PHILEMON

Read the story of Baucis and Philemon.

The first written record of the story of Baucis and Philemon came from a Roman poet named Ovid, born in 43 B.C. Since then, this story like other Greek and Roman myths, has been translated and retold countless times. *The Story of Baucis and Philemon* by Pamela Espeland is one of many versions of this Roman myth.

About 150 A.D., Rome became a very important center of government. As the Roman Empire spread to neighboring countries, they gathered the knowledge and stories of those they conquered. Many of the myths told by the ancient Greeks were rewritten using Roman names for the characters. Zeus, the most important Greek god, became known to the Romans as Jupiter.

Use reference sources to match the Greek and Roman names of these gods and goddesses.

Greek Name	**Roman Name**
_____ Hera, wife of Zeus	A. Mercury
_____ Poseidon, god of the sea	B. Pluto
_____ Aphrodite, goddess of love	C. Mars
_____ Hermes, the messenger god	D. Juno
_____ Hades, god of the underworld	E. Venus
_____ Ares, god of war	F. Neptune

A **myth** is a story that tries to explain nature and the world around us. What does the story of Baucis and Philemon explain?

_____

_____

_____

Ovid wrote his stories in the form of poems. On a separate piece of paper, rewrite this story as a short poem.

Discussion Topics

- Why did Jupiter and Mercury decide to visit the people of Earth?
- Why did they disguise themselves?
- Why did they decide to test the people of the village?
- What happened to all the villagers except Baucis and Philemon? Why?

▖▖▘METAMORPHOSIS

Metamorphosis means "changes." Metamorphosis occurs when a tadpole grows into a frog and when a caterpillar becomes a butterfly.

List three examples of metamorphosis (change) found in the story of Baucis and Philemon.

1. _____

2. _____

3. _____

What Do You Think?

What did Baucis and Philemon ask from the gods?

_____

Why do you think Baucis and Philemon made that request?

_____

What would you have asked for if Jupiter and Mercury had offered to grant you a gift?

_____

Long ago it was customary for travelers to stop and ask for food and shelter. There were no motels and restaurants and few inns for travelers to stay. Sometimes the travelers paid for their food and lodging if they had any money. Usually, they paid by entertaining their hosts, singing or telling stories and bringing them news of far-off places.

Why would news of far-off places be considered payment?

_____

_____

Why did Baucis and Philemon invite the strangers in?

_____

_____

What did they expect in return?

_____

Today it is dangerous to let strangers into our homes, but we can still help others. How can you help others at school? In your neighborhood? In your family?

_____

_____

THE GOLDEN TOUCH

Read "The Golden Touch" by Nathaniel Hawthorne. It is one of many versions of the story about King Midas.

About the Author: Nathaniel Hawthorne was an important American author of the 19th century. He was born in Massachusetts in 1804. After publishing several dozen tales and sketches in newspapers and magazines, he found he could not make enough money as an author. He applied for and received a position at the Boston Custom House. After moving to Concord, he returned to writing.

Between 1849 and 1852 he wrote three novels and a book of short stories. He later wrote a biography of Franklin Pierce, a college friend. President Pierce later appointed Hawthorne as U.S. consul at Liverpool, England. Hawthorne lived in England and Italy for several years while continuing his writing career.

In his writing Hawthorne is noted for the insight he shows into why people behave the way they do. He used allegory and symbolism to develop his own unique style of writing.

Discussion Topics

- What made King Midas happy at the beginning of the story?
- What made King Midas unhappy at the beginning of the story?
- What made Marygold happy?
- What made Marygold unhappy?
- Did the golden touch make King Midas happy? Why or why not?
- What did King Midas think when the handkerchief his daughter made turned to gold?
- King Midas was delighted when he turned the flowers in the garden to gold. How did Marygold feel about the golden flowers?
- What did King Midas learn?

Other Reading

Other works by Nathaniel Hawthorne include *The Scarlet Letter*, *Twice Told Tales* and *The House of the Seven Gables*.

D'Aulaire's Book of Greek Myths written and illustrated by Ingri and Edgar Parin D'Aulaire.

◨ KING MIDAS

At the beginning of the story King Midas thought the best way to show his love for his daughter would be to acquire as much wealth as possible. Do you think his daughter agreed?

_____

Do you agree? Why or why not?

_____

_____

Many gold images (items that are bright yellow or gold) appear in the story. List several of them.

_____   _____   _____

_____   _____   _____

The author notes that ". . . people always grow more and more foolish, unless they take care to grow wiser and wiser . . ." Do you agree or disagree? Why?

_____

_____

"It struck Midas as rather inconvenient that, with all his wealth, he would never again be rich enough to own a pair of serviceable spectacles." Why couldn't he ever have a pair of glasses that he could wear?

_____

_____

Write a moral for this story.

_____

_____

Complete one of these activities:

- What does this saying mean? "Be careful what you ask for; you might get it."
- Illustrate one scene from this story.
- Act out this story in pantomime (without using any words).
- Write a poem based on "The Golden Touch."
- Retell the story from Marygold's point of view.
- Compare "The Golden Touch" to "The Goose That Laid the Golden Egg."

THE MAGIC SHOP

Read "The Magic Shop" by H.G. Wells.

About the Author: Herbert George Wells was born in England in 1866. Wells left school at the age of 14, but returned four years later when he won a scholarship and then a grant to London University. He graduated with a degree in biology in 1890.

He and Jules Verne are usually credited with the invention of the science fiction novel. Wells correctly predicted space exploration, atomic power and other technological developments. At first, Wells firmly believed that science would help create a more perfect world. He later came to believe the human race was likely to destroy itself through technology. Wells died in 1946.

Discussion Topics

- What do you think of the salesman in the Magic Shop?
- Do you think this shop sells "genuine" magic tricks? Why or why not?
- What makes Gip the "right sort of boy"?
- Why are some children not allowed to enter the Magic Shop?
- Why can't the father find the Magic Shop when he looks for it at the end of the story?
- Would you like to visit a magic shop like this one? Why or why not?

Other Reading

Books by H.G. Wells include *The Time Machine, The Invisible Man* and *The War of the Worlds*.

Books by Jules Verne include *Twenty Thousand Leagues Under the Sea* and *Around the World in Eighty Days*.

■ GENUINE MAGIC?

At what point in the story do you get the first clue that the Magic Shop may not be what it seems?

_____

_____

If there were a Magic Shop in your neighborhood, would you be the "right sort of child" to enter? Why or why not?

_____

_____

At times in the story, Gip seems very young, only a toddler. "I read about it in a book," he says, so he must be old enough to read. How old do you think Gip is? Why?

_____

_____

How does the father's view of the Magic Shop differ from Gip's view? Why?

_____

_____

_____

At first, the father thinks the salesman is joking when he says they get all their smaller tricks by picking them out of thin air. Later he's not so sure it was a joke. Why?

_____

_____

_____

What incidents in the story make you believe the magic is real?

_____

_____

Select one of the following activities:

- ■ Learn a magic trick or card trick and demonstrate it for the class.
- ■ Draw a picture of what you think the salesman in the Magic Shop looked liked. Go back to the story and reread the description.
- ■ Compare "The Magic Shop" to another book or story by H.G. Wells.
- ■ Write a report about a well-known magician.
- ■ Write a short story about your visit to a magic shop.

▉ JUST SO STORIES

Read *Just So Stories* by Rudyard Kipling.

About the Author: Born in Bombay, India, in 1865, the Englishman (Joseph) Rudyard Kipling became a noted novelist, short story writer and poet. Kipling was educated in England but returned to India to work as a journalist from 1882 to 1889. Many of the stories, books and poems he wrote after moving back to England are set in India. In 1907, Kipling became the first English writer to win the Nobel Prize for literature.

Kipling wrote *Just So Stories* in 1902 for his daughter, Josephine. Millions of readers, young and old, have enjoyed the tales of how the camel got his hump, how the rhinoceros got his skin and other wonders of the natural world as told in Kipling's playful and original style.

Tell It Like It Is, or Like It Might Have Been

After reading "How the Camel Got His Hump" and "How the Rhinoceros Got His Skin," write your own "Just So" story to explain one of the questions below.

- How the Zebra Got His Stripes
- How the Stars Got in the Sky
- How the Sea Became Salty
- How the Turtle Got His Shell
- How the Beaver Got His Tail
- How the Hummingbird Got So Small
- Why the Ostrich Cannot Fly

- Why the Penguin Has to Waddle
- How the Snake Lost His Legs
- How the Leaves Turned Green
- How the Sheep Got Its Wool
- How the Crow Got Its Caw
- Why the Coyote Howls at the Moon

Prewrite: Write ideas, words and phrases you could use for your story. Write the final version of your story on another sheet of paper. Illustrate your story.

_____

_____

_____

Other Reading

Other "Just So" stories by Rudyard Kipling include "How the Whale Got His Throat," How the Leopard Got His Spots," "The Elephant's Child" and "The Butterfly That Stamped."

He also wrote *The Jungle Book, Kim* and *Captains Courageous*.

HOW THE CAMEL GOT HIS HUMP

Read "How the Camel Got His Hump" by Rudyard Kipling.

Discussion Topics

- Do you think Kipling meant this to be a scientific explanation of why camels have humps? Why or why not?
- Why do you think some words in the story are capitalized that usually aren't?
- Why did the dog and the horse and the ox complain about the camel?
- What is a Djinn?
- What happens when the Djinn warns the camel not to say *humph* again?
- Why does the Djinn tell the camel he brought the humph on himself?
- The author doesn't tell us what the camel had to say after the Djinn put the humph on his back. What do you think the camel said?
- Do you think the camel deserved his humph?
- If you had been the Djinn, what would you have done about the camel?
- Do you feel sorry for the camel? Why or why not?
- What is the purpose of the humph on the camel's back?
- Did the camel learn his lesson at the end of the story?
- Why do we call it a hump instead of a humph?
- What would be a good moral for this story?

Picture It

In the box below, draw or paint a picture of the Djinn or of a camel without a hump.

HOW THE RHINOCEROS GOT HIS SKIN

Read "How the Rhinoceros Got His Skin" by Rudyard Kipling.

Explain why is it impossible for someone to live on an **uninhabited** island.

_____

Why do you think the Parsee climbed up the palm tree when the rhinoceros came and ate his cake?

_____

How did the Parsee man's first poem foretell what would happen to the rhinoceros?

_____

Why did the Parsee smile a smile that "ran around his face two times" when he saw the rhinoceros's skin on the bank of the river?

_____

Why did the Parsee put "old, dry tickly cake-crumbs and some burned currants" inside the rhinoceros's skin?

_____

_____

Complete one of the following activities:

- Draw a rhinoceros with a tight-fitting skin.

- Draw a rhinoceros bathing without his skin.

- Draw a Parsee man with a hat that reflected the rays of the sun "in more-than-oriental splendour."

- Make up a story about how the rhinoceros got his horn.

- Write a rhyming poem about how the rhinoceros got his skin.

- Write a limerick about how the rhinoceros felt when he put on his skin with the crumbs inside.

- Draw a map showing the location of the uninhabited island where the Parsee lived. Include the "Exclusively Uninhabited Interior" and the "islands of Mazanderan, Socotta and the Promontories of the Larger Equinox." Include also "Orotavo, Amygdala, the Upland Meadows of Anantarivo and the Marshes of Sonaput." Feel free to add the names of other important places and seas on your map.

O CAPTAIN! MY CAPTAIN!

Read "O Captain! My Captain!" by Walt Whitman below.

Walt Whitman wrote "O Captain! My Captain!" after the assassination of Abraham Lincoln five days after the end of the Civil War in 1865.

O Captain! My Captain!

O Captain! My Captain! our fearful trip is done,
The ship has weathered every rack, the prize we sought is won,
The port is near, the bells I hear, the people all exulting,
While follow eyes the steady keel, the vessel grim and daring:
    But O heart! heart! heart!
      O the bleeding drops of red,
        Where on the deck my Captain lies,
          Fallen cold and dead.

O Captain! My Captain! rise up and hear the bells:
Rise up—for you the flag is flug—for you the bugle trills,
For you bouquets and ribboned wreaths—for you the shores acrowding,
For you they call, the swaying mass, their eager faces turning;
    Hear captain! dear father!
      The arm beneath your head!
        It is some dream that on the deck,
          You've fallen cold and dead.

My Captain does not answer, his lips are pale and still,
My father does not feel my arm, he has no pulse nor will,
The ship is anchored safe and sound, its voyage closed and done,
From fearful trip the victor ship comes in with object won:
    Exult O shores, and ring O bells!
      But I with mournful tread,
        Walk the deck my captain lies,
          Fallen cold and dead.

About the Author: Walt Whitman, born in 1819, grew up in Brooklyn, New York. He began learning the printing trade when he was 11. During his career he held jobs as a printer, journalist, school teacher, writer and newspaper editor. For a time he assisted his father in the building business. During the Civil War he worked in various government departments and as a volunteer at a hospital for wounded soldiers.

Today, many believe Whitman was the greatest 19th century American poet. *Leaves of Grass*, Whitman's first book of poems contained only nine poems when it was first published in 1855. He continuously revised his book and added new poems. The ninth edition, published shortly before his death, contained 400 poems.

Whitman's poetry was not widely accepted at first because he did not use traditional poetic forms and meter. He wrote about commonplace events, democracy, freedom, the self and the joys of living.

THE SHIP

A metaphor is a figure of speech that compares two unlike items without using the words *like* or *as*.

Whitman uses several metaphors in "O Captain! My Captain!" He compares the United States to a ship and Abraham Lincoln to the captain. The ship has been on a terrible journey, the Civil War.

What do you think Whitman meant by these phrases:

"the prize we sought" _____

_____

"the port is near"_____

_____

"the steady keel" _____

_____

"the vessel grim and daring" _____

_____

"dear father" _____

_____

"the victor ship" _____

_____

"object won" _____

_____

Think About and Discuss

■ Although Lincoln was only three years older than Whitman, Whitman calls him "father." Why?

■ Whitman appears to want to deny the truth, that Lincoln has been killed. What phrases in the poem show that? Why would he use those phrases? Did you like this poem? Why or why not?

■ How do you think Whitman felt about Lincoln's death?

■ Find examples of words Whitman uses that show this poem is very personal. What is the difference between a personal poem and an objective poem?

■ If a poet wrote about the death of a great leader today, what types of metaphors could be used instead of a ship? Give some examples.

Write your answer to one of the above questions.

_____

_____

■ "O CAPTAIN! MY CAPTAIN" ACTIVITIES

Complete the assigned activities.

- ■ Which line in this poem do you like best? Why?
- ■ Rewrite this poem as a short story or newspaper article.
- ■ Compare the tone in the first three lines of the first verse to the first three lines of the last verse.
- ■ Write a short biography of Abraham Lincoln.
- ■ Write about events during the Civil War.
- ■ Write a poem about Abraham Lincoln.
- ■ Write a poem about the Civil War.
- ■ Use metaphors to write a poem about a person.
- ■ Do an illustration or collage for this poem.
- ■ Whitman was the first major poet to use free verse for poetry. What is free verse?
- ■ Compare "O Captain! My Captain!" to another poem by Walt Whitman.
- ■ Compare "O Captain! My Captain!" to another poem about Abraham Lincoln.
- ■ Compare "O Captain! My Captain!" to another poem by a writer of the same time period.

Rewrite the first verse of the poem without any metaphors.

_____

_____

_____

_____

_____

_____

_____

_____

Other **R**eading

"I Hear America Singing" by Walt Whitman.

"Lincoln" by Nancy Byrd Turner.

"Abraham Lincoln Walks at Midnight" by Vachel Lindsay.

Oxford Book of Poetry for Children Edited by Edward Bilshen.

Leaves of Grass: *Selections from a Great Poetic Work* by Walt Whitman.

Name _____

⬛ IN JUST

Read the poem "in Just" by e e cummings.

Did you like this poem? Why or why not?

_____

_____

Look at the spacing of the words *whistles far and wee* the three times they appear in the poem. What do you think the whistle of the balloonman stands for?

_____

_____

What do you think the different word spacing means?

_____

_____

Is the balloonman getting closer or farther away at the end of the poem? Explain your answer.

_____

Why do you think cummings used a balloonman in this poem?

_____

About the Author: His pen name was e e cummings. Born in Cambridge, Massachusetts, in 1894, his real name was Edward Estin Cummings.

After receiving his bachelor's and master's degree in English from Harvard, cummings volunteered for the ambulance corps in France during World War I. Because he criticized the war, the French arrested him and sent him to a detention center for three months. He wrote about his prison camp experiences in his first published book, *The Enormous Room*. When he returned to the United States, he was drafted into the Army. Many of his poems are satires on military life.

After the war he turned to a career as a writer and artist, publishing 11 books of poetry, several plays, journals, essays and a group of children's stories titled *Fairy Tales* written for his daughter.

Although many of his verses were written in traditional style and meter, cummings is best known for the lack of punctuation and capitalization found in so many of his poems. He became famous for using unusual grammar, spacing and word order in his poems.

Other Reading

100 selected poems by e e cummings.

Street Poems by Robert Froman.

▌ "IN JUST" ACTIVITIES

Complete the assigned activities.

- In Greek mythology, Pan was portrayed with the body of a man and the legs of a goat. Learn more about Pan. Why did e e cummings use the image of Pan for the balloonman?

- The first time the balloonman is mentioned, he is described as the little lame balloonman. The second time, he is the queer (meaning "strange") old balloonman, and the final time he is the goat-footed balloonman. Do you think the balloonman stands for good or evil? Does the image of the balloonman change from the beginning of the poem to the end?

- Why do you think cummings didn't put spaces between words like *eddieandbill* and *bettyandisbel*?

- How are the phrases "mud-luscious" and "puddle-wonderful" great descriptions of spring? Write other phrases that describe spring.

- Which word best describes this poem: *lonely, happy, sad, scary* or *funny*? Why?

- What do you think this poem means? Write a summary of this poem.

- Compare this poem to the story of the Pied Piper of Hamelin.

- Read another poem by e e cummings and compare it to "in Just."

- Illustrate "in Just" or another poem by e e cummings.

Discussion Topics

- Read the poem aloud. How does the spacing of the words and the breaks in the line influence your reading?

- What do you think about poetry that rarely uses capital letters or punctuation? Is it confusing?

- How does the spacing of the words affect the meaning of the poem?

- What does the word *just* mean in this poem?

- Is there anything eerie about the balloonman?

THE OLD MAN WITH A BEARD

There was an Old Man with a beard,
Who said, "It is just as I feared!—
Two Owls and a Hen,
Four Larks and a Wren,
Have all built their nests in my beard!"

About the Author: Edward Lear was born on May 12, 1812. He was the twentieth of 21 children. His first *Book of Nonsense* was published in 1846.

Edward Lear became Queen Victoria's drawing master for a time. In 1832 he was commissioned by the Earl of Derby to illustrate a book about the Earl's private zoo which contained 500 animals and 1700 birds. Although Lear was an accomplished artist, cartoonist and landscape painter, he is best remembered for his illustrated nonsense verses and limericks.

Discussion Topics

- Did you like this poem? Why or why not?
- Is this poem humorous? Why or why not?
- Do you like limericks? Why or why not?
- Should poetry only be about serious topics? Explain your answer.

Complete the assigned activities.

- Why are limericks fun poems?
- Lear's poems are often called whimsical. What does *whimsical* mean? Why are his poems called whimsical?
- Compare "The Old Man with a Beard" to another limerick by Edward Lear.
- Illustrate "The Old Man with a Beard" or another poem by Edward Lear.
- Write a short report about Edward Lear's life.
- Imagine being the twentieth of 21 children. Write a limerick about living in a large family.
- Study several of Edward Lear's illustrations. What do you think of his drawings? Was he a better poet or artist?
- How do his illustrations enhance his poems?

Other Reading

Besides other limericks by Edward Lear, you might enjoy some of his longer poems like "The Owl and the Pussycat," "The Quangle Wangle's Hat" and "The Table and the Chair."

How Pleasant to Know Mr. Lear! by Edward Lear.

Loony Limericks from Alabama to Wyoming written and illustrated by Jack Stokes.

▌WRITING A LIMERICK

Limericks are five-line poems that are fun to read and write.

Limerick rhyme pattern:

Lines 1, 2 and 5 rhyme.

Lines 3 and 4 rhyme and are shorter.

What is the last word in each line of "The Old Man with a Beard"?

Line 1 _____

Line 2 _____

Line 3 _____

Line 4 _____

Line 5 _____

In many limericks, the last word in line five is the same as the last word in line one.

In Edward Lear's limericks, the first line usually introduced a character.

"There was an Old Man with a beard,"
"There was an Old Lady of France,"
"There was a Young Lady of Welling,"
"There was an Old Man of Three Bridges,"

Read other limericks for more examples.

Write your own limerick about a person. Introduce the character in the first line. Use the limerick rhyme pattern. Illustrate your limerick in a cartoon style.

_____ *(title)*

_____

_____

_____

_____

POEMS BY OGDEN NASH

Copy the two short poems "The Camel" and "The Lama" below.

The Camel

_____

_____

_____

_____

About the Author: Although he didn't use his first name, his full name was Frederic Ogden Nash. He was born in Rye, New York, in 1902 and published hundreds of humorous verses. Most of his poems were written in rhymed couplets (two lines that rhyme). Many of his poems, like "The Lama" use a play on words. Besides writing 19 books of poetry, Nash also coauthored a successful musical comedy, *One Touch of Venus,* in 1943.

The Lama

_____

_____

_____

_____

_____

_____

_____

_____

Discussion Topics

- Did you like these two poems by Ogden Nash? Why or why not?
- Which of the poems did you like better? Why?
- Do you think these poems were meant to be taken seriously? Why or why not?
- Are these two poems funny? Why or why not?

Other Reading

Versus and *You Can't Get There from Here* by Ogden Nash.

Hurry, Hurry, Mary Dear! And Other Nonsense by N.M. Bodecker.

A Great Big Ugly Man Came Up and Tied His Horse to Me: A Book of Nonsense Verse by Wallace Tripp.

Where the Sidewalk Ends: Poems and Drawings by Shel Silverstein.

THE CAMEL AND THE LAMA

In the box below, write a short comparison poem about two animals in the same style used by Ogden Nash in "The Camel." You could compare tigers and house cats, African and Indian elephants, Great Danes and dachshunds, whales and minnows, turtles and tortoises, ostriches and hummingbirds or any other two birds, fish or animals. Don't forget to title your poem.

Complete the assigned activities.

- Illustrate one of these two poems.
- What is the difference between a camel and a dromedary?
- Use a dictionary to define *lama* and *llama*. Make up a definition for *llama*. Illustrate one of these words.
- Write a short report about Ogden Nash's life.
- Compare and contrast "The Camel" and "The Lama."
- Compare one of these poems to a limerick by Edward Lear.
- Define the term *a play on words*. The title of one of Ogden Nash's poetry books is *Versus*. How is that title a play on words?
- Write a short poem that uses wordplay. You could use a set of homonyms like *blew* and *blue*; *tale* and *tail*; *sew, so* and *sow*; *pane* and *pain*; *which* and *witch* or *wear* and *where* for your play on words.
- Write a poem using several couplets (two lines of a poem that rhyme).

Name _____

⬛ THE RED WHEELBARROW

On the lines below, copy the poem "The Red Wheelbarrow" by William Carlos Williams.

The Red Wheelbarrow

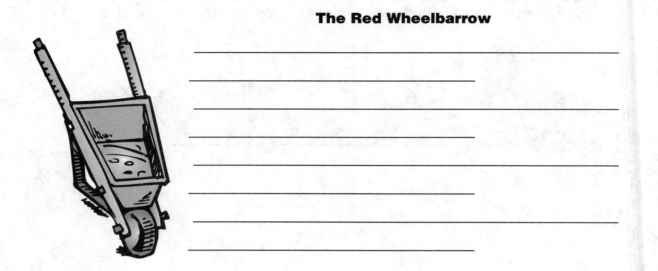

_____

_____

_____

_____

_____

_____

About the Author: Born in Rutherford, New York, in 1883, William Carlos Williams became an original, imaginative American poet, interested in new ways to express timeless truths. His poems are filled with images of people and nature.

After graduating from medical school in 1906, Williams became a pediatrician in his hometown. He published his first book, *Poems*, three years later. Williams wrote nearly 40 other books of poetry, fiction, plays, essays, biography and autobiography while continuing his career as a doctor. He died in 1963.

Illustrate the Poem

How do you visualize the red wheelbarrow? Is it bright, shiny red? Is it old and weathered with the paint peeling off? Illustrate your image of this poem.

◧ YOUR POEM

Write a poem in this same style and meter, starting with the same words William Carlos Williams used. Use alternating lines of three words and one word.

so much depends
upon

_____   _____   _____

_____

_____   _____   _____

_____   _____   _____

_____   _____   _____

_____

What is the title of your poem?_____

Illustrate your poem.

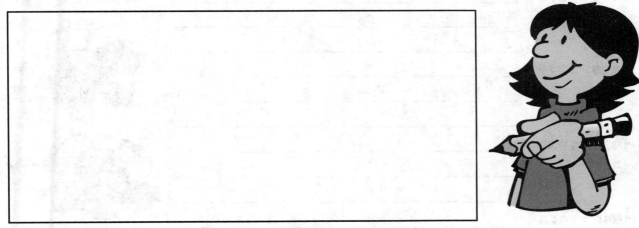

Why did you select that item to describe in your poem?

_____

_____

_____

Compare your poem to "The Red Wheelbarrow."

_____

DURING HIS LIFETIME

Think of all the changes Williams saw during his life (1883-1963), like the invention of the automobile and the airplane. Imagine all the historical events that occurred during his lifetime, like the Great Depression, World War I and World War II. Who was the President of the United States the year William Carlos Williams was born? Who was the President of the United States the year he died?

For the time line below, fill in important events that occurred during his life.

1883 - 1889 _____
_____
_____

1890 - 1899 _____
_____
_____

1900 - 1909 _____
_____
_____

1910 - 1919 _____
_____
_____

1920 - 1929 _____
_____
_____

1930 - 1939 _____
_____
_____

1940 - 1949 _____
_____
_____

1950 - 1959 _____
_____
_____

1960 - 1963 _____
_____
_____

▮ HAIKU

Haiku poetry originated in Japan. Each poem consists of three unrhymed lines. Each line has a specific number of syllables:

Line 1 = 5 syllables
Line 2 = 7 syllables
Line 3 = 5 syllables

Many haiku poems are written about nature or one of the four seasons. Here are two examples:

A Sign of Spring   Number of Syllables

Two lonely robins   _____

Shivering. Searching through March   _____

For a sign of spring.   _____

They Are Dust

Dinosaurs once ruled   _____

The Earth as Masters of all.   _____

Today they are dust.   _____

Count the syllables and write the number at the end of each line.

Select a topic you would like to write about. It could be a season, a wild animal or a pet, the wind, rain or snow. You could write about a plant or a tree, a forest, a jungle or an ocean.

Prewrite: Write words about the topic you could use in your poem.

_____   _____   _____

_____   _____   _____

Work on scrap paper to start your haiku poem. Choose your words carefully. Every syllable counts. Rewrite your poem as many times as you need to until you are satisfied with it. Count the number of syllables in each line. When you're finished, write your poem below. Don't forget the title.

_____

_____

_____

_____

Other Reading

A Few Flies and I Haiku verses selected by Jean Merril and Ronni Solbert.

Cricket Songs: Japanese Haiku Translated by Harry Behn.

THE BELLS

Read "The Bells" by Edgar Allan Poe.

I

Hear the sledges with the bells—
   Silver bells!
What a world of merriment their melody foretells!
How they tinkle, tinkle, tinkle,
  In the icy air of night!
While the stars that oversprinkle
All the heavens, seem to twinkle
  With a crystalline delight;
    Keeping time, time, time,
    In a sort of Runic rhyme,
To the tintinnabulation that so musically wells
    From the bells, bells, bells, bells,
     Bells, bells, bells—
From the jingling and the tinkling of the bells.

II

Hear the mellow wedding bells,
   Golden bells!
What a world of happiness their harmony foretells!
  Through the balmy air of night
How they ring out their delight!—
   From the molten-golden notes,
    And all in tune,
  What a liquid ditty floats
To the turtle-dove that listens, while she gloats
   On the moon!
  Oh, from out the sounding cells,
What a gush of euphony voluminously wells!
   How it swells!
   How it dwells
   On the Future!—how it tells
   Of the rapture that impels
  To the swinging and the ringing
   Of the bells, bells, bells—
Of the bells, bells, bells, bells,
    Bells, bells, bells—
To the rhyming and the chiming of the bells!

III

Hear the loud alarum bells—
   Brazen bells!
What a tale of terror, now, their turbulency tells!
  In the startled ear of night
How they scream out their affright!

   Too much horrified to speak,
   They can only shriek, shriek,
    Out of tune,
In a clamorous appealing to the mercy of the fire,
In a mad expostulation with the deaf and frantic fire,
    Leaping higher, higher, higher,
    With a desperate desire,
  And a resolute endeavor,
  Now—now to sit, or never,
By the side of the pale-faced moon.
   Oh the bells, bells, bells!
   What a tale their terror tells
    Of Despair!
   How they clang, and clash, and roar!
   What a horror they outpour
On the bosom of the palpitating air!
   Yet the ear it fully knows,
    By the twanging,
    And the clanging,
   How the danger ebbs and flows;
  Yet the ear distinctly tells,
    In the jangling,
    And the wrangling,
  How the danger sinks and swells,
By the sinking or the swelling in the anger of the bells—
     Of the bells—
  Of the bells, bells, bells, bells,
    Bells, bells bells—
In the clamor and the clangor of the bells!

◼ THE BELLS

IV

Hear the tolling of the bells—
    Iron bells!
What a world of solemn thought their monody com-
pels!
  In the silence of the night,
  How we shiver with affright
At the melancholy menace of their tone!
  For every sound that floats
  From the rust within their throats
    Is a groan.
    And the people—ah, the people—
    They that dwell up in the steeple,
    All alone,
    And who, tolling, tolling, tolling,
    In that muffled monotone,
    Feel a glory in so rolling
      On the human heart a stone—
    They are neither man nor woman—
    They are neither brute nor human—
     They are Ghouls:—
    And their king it is who tolls:—
    And he rolls, rolls, rolls,
    Rolls
     A paean from the bells!
    And his merry bosom swells
     With the paean of the bells!
    And he dances, and he yells;

Keeping time, time, time,
In a sort of Runic rhyme,
    To the paean of the bells—
    Of the bells:
Keeping time, time, time,
In a sort of Runic rhyme,
    To the throbbing of the bells—
   Of the bells, bells, bells—
    To the sobbing of the bells:
  Keeping time, time, time,
   As he knells, knells, knells,
  In a happy Runic rhyme,
    To the rolling of the bells—
   Of the bells, bells, bells:—
    To the tolling of the bells,
   Of the bells, bells, bells, bells—
    Bells, bells, bells—
To the moaning and the groaning of the bells.

THE BELLS

About the Author: Edgar Allan Poe was orphaned before he was 3. He moved from Boston where he was born in 1809 to live with John and Frances Allan in Richmond, Virginia. They moved to England when Poe was 6. He attended school there for a time, then continued his education back in Richmond. He attended the University of Virginia, then West Point but did not finish at either school. After his foster mother died, Mr. Allan disinherited him. Although he had already published 36 poems, at the age of 22 he found himself without money or a job.

Poe worked for a time as a magazine editor and book reviewer. He began writing unusual short stories, especially detective stories, a type of fiction almost unknown at that time. "The Murder in the Rue Morgue" and "The Purloined Letter" focus the reader's attention on the brilliant detective logic used to solve the crime. Poe's career as a writer was short. He died at the age of 40.

Poe is remembered for his musical poetry as well as his stories that deal with the mysterious, the strange and the dark side of human nature.

The Bells: What metals and images does Poe use for each type of bell?

I Sleigh bells: _____   **II** Wedding bells: _____

_____   _____

III Alarm bells: _____   **IV** Funeral bells: _____

_____   _____

Why do you think Poe repeated words, especially the words *bells* and *time* in this poem?

_____

In Only One Word: Select one word from each section of "The Bells" that best describes that section.

Section **I:** _____   Section **II:** _____

Section **III:** _____   Section **IV:** _____

Other Reading

"The Raven" and "Annabel Lee" are other poems by Edgar Allan Poe. "The Gold Bug," "The Telltale Heart," "The Black Cat," "The Pit and the Pendulum" and the "Masque of the Red Death" are some of Poe's best-known stories.

◼ WHAT'S THAT NOISE?

slush   squash   ka-plunk   creak   shhhh

whoosh   hummmm   blub   clang   achoo   buzzzzz

A word or group of words that imitates a sound is called **onomatopoeia**. In his poem "The Bells," Edgar Allan Poe writes about the "tintinnabulation" of the bells. Does *tintinnabulation* sound like ringing bells?

_____

List other words in "The Bells" that are onomatopoetic.

_____   _____   _____

_____   _____   _____

Write words or groups of words that imitate the sounds listed below. You can use real words or made-up words.

The sound of a blustery wind on a dark cold night: _____

The sound of windshield wipers when it's raining hard: _____

The sound of wet boots on a dry floor: _____

The sound of a rusty zipper:_____

The sound of water dripping from a tree:_____

The sound of a rotten apple falling from a tree: _____

The sound of a sneeze in a metal garbage can: _____

The sound of a creaky rocking chair: _____

The sound of rain on a tent: _____

The sound of a happy baby: _____

The sound of 10 people eating potato chips: _____

The sound in a seashell when you put it to your ear:_____

Feelings

What do you feel as you read this poem? Read "The Bells" a second time. Stop and describe the feelings you have as you read.

_____

Name _____

▒ STOPPING BY WOODS ON A SNOWY EVENING

Read the poem "Stopping by Woods on a Snowy Evening" by Robert Frost.

Look at the Pattern: Study the rhyme pattern in this poem. In the first verse, lines 1, 2 and 4 rhyme. What does the last word in line 3 rhyme with?

_____

_____

Look at the second and third verses. What is the rhyme pattern?

_____

_____

How does this rhyme pattern link one verse to the next?

_____

_____

How is the rhyme pattern different in the last verse? Why is it different?

_____

_____

About the Author: Although Frost was born in San Francisco in 1874, his family moved to Massachusetts in 1885 after his father died. Many of his poems are set in rural New England. He attended college for a time, then worked in a mill, ran a farm, worked as a reporter, taught school and wrote poetry.

While he and his family lived in England (1912-1915), Frost began publishing his poetry. When they returned to the United States, they moved to a farm in New Hampshire where Frost continued writing, teaching and lecturing.

Robert Frost is one of America's most widely read poets whose works combine a lyrical (musical) quality with philosophical tones. He received four Pulitzer Prizes and many other honors for his poetry during his lifetime. Robert Frost died in 1963.

Other Reading

You Come Too: Favorite Poems for Young Readers by Robert Frost.

A Swinger of Birches: Poems of Robert Frost for Young People by Robert Frost.

◼ YOUR IMPRESSION

What one word sums up your impression of this poem? _____

What do you know about the speaker from reading the poem?

_____

Why did the speaker stop by the woods?

_____

The speaker sounds sad in the last verse. Why do you think the speaker is sad?

_____

What might be the promises the speaker has to keep? Do you think the promises have anything to do with the last two lines? Explain your answer.

_____

Describe how you would feel if you had to leave a beautiful, restful place before you were ready because you had promised to be somewhere else.

_____

_____

_____

Did you like this poem? Why or why not?

_____

_____

Do an illustration of this poem or of how the poem makes you feel.

FATHER WILLIAM

"You are old, Father William," the young man said,
  "And your hair has become very white;
And yet you incessantly stand on your head—
  Do you think, at your age, it is right?"

"In my youth," Father William replied to his son,
  "I feared it might injure the brain;
But, now that I'm perfectly sure I have none,
  Why, I do it again and again."

"You are old," said the youth, "as I mentioned before.
  And have grown most uncommonly fat;
Yet you turned a back-somersault in at the door—
  Pray, what is the reason of that?"

"In my youth," said the sage, as he shook his grey locks,
  "I kept all my limbs very supple
By the use of this ointment — one shilling the box—
  Allow me to sell you a couple?"

"You are old," said the youth, "and your jaws are too weak
  For anything tougher than suet;
Yet you finished the goose, with the bones and the beak—
  Pray, how did you manage to do it?"

"In my youth," said his father, "I took to the law,
  And argued each case with my wife;
And the muscular strength which it gave to my jaw
  Has lasted the rest of my life."

"You are old," said the youth, "one would hardly suppose
  That your eye was as steady as ever;
Yet you balanced an eel on the end of your nose—
  What made you so awfully clever?"

"I have answered three questions, and that is enough,"
  Said his father. "Don't give yourself airs!
Do you think I can listen all day to such stuff?
  Be off, or I'll kick you downstairs!"

About the Author: Lewis Carroll is the pen name used by the English writer Charles Dodgson, born in 1832. The oldest of 11 children, Lewis Carroll graduated from the University at Oxford and became a clergyman, mathematician and author. He is best known for his book *Alice's Adventures in Wonderland* and for several short nonsense poems.

Assignment: Did this poem make you laugh? If you answered "yes," read it again just for fun. If you answered "no," write a 10,000-page essay on the history of humor from 55 million B.C. to the present—or read the poem again and try to find a chuckle somewhere.

Pizza Deluxe: Cut a 3'-4' (.91-1.2 m) diameter circle from brown or white paper. Color it to look like a pizza covered with sauce and cheese. Cut out shapes for pepperoni, mushrooms and green pepper strips. (Students could do this as an art project.) Each shape should be large enough to allow students to write their names and the title of a book on it. When students have finished reading a book, allow them to select one of the shapes and add it to the pizza. Hold a pizza party to kick off the project or celebrate when the pizza is filled with books read.

Read-o-Meter: Divide the class into two or more groups. For each group, cut a 3' x 8" (.91m x 20.32 cm) sheet of paper or poster board. Label each Read-o-Meter. Divide the Read-o-Meters by inches (centimeters), vertically and label them from 1 to 36. For each book a student reads, she can write her name and book title in a 1" (2.54 cm) space and color it in. The first group to fill all 36 spaces receives some type of reward, like a bag of powdered sugar doughnuts, popcorn, cookies, snack cakes or a special privilege.

Poet"tree": Get a large, bare tree branch with many smaller branches still attached. Set it upright in a bucket of sand or gravel. Have students write short poems on leaf-shaped pieces of paper and add them to the poet"tree." Poems could be original ones or ones the students have read and enjoyed. Pick different poems from the tree each day to read aloud.

Hang 'Em up for All to See: String a clothesline along a wall in your class. Cut construction paper in the shape of an open book. For each book students read, they can write their name, book title and author on one side. On the other side, they can write a short summary of the book. Attach the completed book shapes to your clothesline with colored plastic clothespins.

World Map: Display a large world map on the bulletin board. Use a colored pushpin to mark the location of the story for each book students read. Use a small label to number the pins. Put a numbered map key nearby. Write the title of the book next to the appropriate number.

Love to Read: Cut a large paper heart from red construction paper. Write the words *Love to Read* on the heart in large letters. Cut lots of smaller hearts from red, white and pink construction paper. As students finish reading books, they can write their names and the book titles on the smaller hearts and add them in a display around the large heart.

Five-Star Books: Cut out construction paper stars. When a student finishes reading a book, he can write his name and the book title on a star, then add the appropriate number (one to five) of star stickers to rate the book. Display the stars on your bulletin board, window or ceiling.

OLYMPIC READER AWARD

This is to certify that _____

has completed the Olympic Pentathlon
by reading books in the following five categories:

Book Title

___ **A**dventure   _____

___ **A**utobiography   _____

___ **B**iography   _____

___ **C**ontemporary fiction   _____

___ **D**rama   _____

___ **F**antasy   _____

___ **F**olklore   _____

___ **H**istorical fiction   _____

___ **H**umor   _____

___ **I**nternational   _____

___ **M**ulticultural   _____

___ **M**ystery   _____

___ **M**yths, fables or legends   _____

___ **N**onfiction   _____

___ **P**oetry   _____

___ **S**cience   _____

___ **S**cience fiction   _____

___ **S**hort story anthology   _____

___ **S**ports   _____

___ **T**all tales   _____

___ **W**estern   _____

Signature of Olympic Judge: _____

Date: _____

OLYMPIC READER AWARD

This is to certify that _____

has completed the Olympic Pentathlon
by reading books in the following five categories:

Book Title

___ **A**dventure   _____

___ **A**utobiography   _____

___ **B**iography   _____

___ **C**ontemporary fiction   _____

___ **D**rama   _____

___ **F**antasy   _____

___ **F**olklore   _____

___ **H**istorical fiction   _____

___ **H**umor   _____

___ **I**nternational   _____

___ **M**ulticultural   _____

___ **M**ystery   _____

___ **M**yths, fables or legends   _____

___ **N**onfiction   _____

___ **P**oetry   _____

___ **S**cience   _____

___ **S**cience fiction   _____

___ **S**hort story anthology   _____

___ **S**ports   _____

___ **T**all tales   _____

___ **W**estern   _____

Signature of Olympic Judge: _____

Date: _____

SUGGESTED POETRY READING

A Few Flies and I Haiku verses selected by Jean Merril and Ronni Solbert (Pantheon Books, 1969).

A Book of Animal Poems Selected by William Cole (Viking, 1973).

Bilshen, Edward. Editor. *Oxford Book of Poetry for Children* (Franklin Watts, 1963).

Bodecker, N.M. *Hurry, Hurry, Mary Dear! And Other Nonsense* (Atheneum, 1979).

Cricket Songs: Japanese Haiku Translated by Harry Behn (Harcourt, 1964).

cummings, e e. *100 selected poems* (Grove Press, Inc., 1954).

Froman, Robert. *Street Poems* (McCall, 1971).

Frost, Robert. *A Swinger of Birches: Poems of Robert Frost for Young People* (Holt, Rinehart and Winston, 1982).

Frost, Robert. *You Come Too: Favorite Poems for Young Readers* (Holt and Company, 1959).

Giroux, Joan. *The Haiku Form* (Charles E. Tuttle Company, 1974).

Hall, Donald, Editor. *The Oxford Book of Children's Verse in America* (Oxford University Press, 1985).

How to Eat a Poem and Other Morsels Selected by Rose Agree (Pantheon Books, 1967).

Lear, Edward. *How Pleasant to Know Mr. Lear!* (Holiday House, 1972).

My Tang's Tungled and Other Ridiculous Situations Compiled by Sara Brewton (Crowell, 1973).

Stokes, Jack. *Loony Limericks from Alabama to Wyoming* (Doubleday, 1978).

The Trees Stand Shining: Poetry of the North American Indian Selected by Hettie Jones (Dial, 1971).

Tripp, Wallace. *A Great Big Ugly Man Came Up and Tied His Horse to Me: A Book of Nonsense Verse* (Little, 1973).

Whitman, Walt. *Leaves of Grass: Selections from a Great Poetic Work* (Avon Books, 1969).

NEWBERY MEDAL AWARD WINNERS

The Newbery Medal is awarded annually by the Association for Library Service to Children, a division of the American Library Association, to the author of the most distinguished contribution to American literature for children.

1922 *The Story of Mankind.* Hendrik Willem van Loon

1923 *The Voyages of Dr. Dolittle.* Hugh Lofting

1924 *The Dark Frigate.* Charles Boardman Hawes

1925 *Tales from Silver Lands.* Charles Joseph Finger

1926 *Shen of the Sea.* Arthur Bowie Chrisman

1927 *Smoky, the Cowhorse.* Will James

1928 *Gay-Neck.* Dhan Gopal Mukerji

1929 *The Trumpeter of Krakow.* Eric P. Kelly

1930 *Hitty, Her First Hundred Years.* Rachel Field

1931 *The Cat Who Went to Heaven.* Elizabeth Coatsworth

1932 *Waterless Mountain.* Laura Adams Armer

1933 *Young Fu of the Upper Yangtze.* Elizabeth Foreman Lewis

1934 *Invincible Louisa.* Cornelia Lynde Meigs

1935 *Dobry.* Monica Shannon

1936 *Caddie Woodlawn.* Carol Ryrie Brink

1937 *Roller Skates.* Ruth Sawyer

1938 *The White Stag.* Kate Seredy

1939 *Thimble Summer.* Elizabeth Enright

1940 *Daniel Boone.* James Daugherty

1941 *Call It Courage.* Armstrong Sperry

1942 *The Matchlock Gun.* Walter D. Edmonds

1943 *Adam of the Road.* Elizabeth Janet Gray

1944 *Johnny Tremain.* Esther Forbes

1945 *Rabbit Hill.* Robert Lawson

1946 *Strawberry Girl.* Lois Lenski

1947 *Miss Hickory.* Carolyn S. Bailey

1948 *The Twenty-One Balloons.* William Péne du Bois

1949 *King of the Wind.* Marguerite Henry

1950 *The Door in the Wall.* Marguerite de Angeli

1951 *Amos Fortune, Free Man.* Elizabeth Yates

1952 *Ginger Pye.* Eleanor Estes

1953 *Secret of the Andes.* Ann Nolan Clark

1954 *. . . and Now Miguel.* Joseph Krumgold

1955 *The Wheels on the School.* Meindert DeJong

1956 *Carry On, Mr. Bowditch.* Jean Lee Latham

1957 *Miracles on Maple Hill.* Virginia Sorenson

1958 *Rifles for Watie.* Harold Keith.

1959 *The Witch of Blackbird Pond.* Elizabeth George Speare

1960 *Onion John.* Joseph Krumgold

1961 *Island of the Blue Dolphins.* Scott O'Dell

1962 *The Bronze Bow.* Elizabeth George Speare

1963 *A Wrinkle in Time.* Madeleine L'Engle

1964 *It's Like This, Cat.* Emily Cheney Neville

1965 *Shadow of a Bull.* Maia Wojciechowska

1966 *I, Juan de Pareja.* Elizabeth B. de Treviño

1967 *Up a Road Slowly.* Irene Hunt

1968 *From the Mixed-Up Files of Mrs. Basil E. Frankweiler.* E.L. Konigsburg

1969 *The High King.* Lloyd Alexander

1970 *Sounder.* William H. Armstrong

1971 *The Summer of the Swans.* Betsy Byars

1972 *Mrs. Frisby and the Rats of NIMH.* Robert C. O'Brien

1973 *Julie of the Wolves.* Jean George

1974 *The Slave Dancer.* Paula Fox

1975 *M.C. Higgins, the Great.* Virgina Hamilton

1976 *Grey King.* Susan Cooper

1977 *Roll of Thunder, Hear My Cry.* Mildred D. Taylor

1978 *Bridge to Terabithia.* Katherine Paterson

1979 *The Westing Game.* Ellen Raskin

1980 *A Gathering of Days.* Joan Blos

1981 *Jacob Have I Loved.* Katherine Paterson

1982 *A Visit to William Blake's Inn: Poems for Innocent and Experienced Travelers.* Nancy Willard.

1983 *Dicey's Song.* Cynthia Voight

1984 *Dear Mr. Henshaw.* Beverly Cleary

1985 *The Hero and the Crown.* Robin McKinley

1986 *Sarah, Plain and Tall.* Patricia MacLachlan

1987 *The Whipping Boy.* Sid Fleischman

1988 *Lincoln: A Photobiography.* Russell Freedman

1989 *Joyful Noise: Poems for Two Voices.* Paul Fleischman

1990 *Number the Stars.* Lois Lowry

1991 *Maniac Magee.* Jerry Spinelli

1992 *Shiloh.* Reynolds Naylor

1993 *Missing May.* Cynthia Ryland

1994 *The Giver.* Lois Lowry

Vocabulary Scavenger Hunt (page 8)

1. nuance
2. minuscule
3. coalition
4. feign
5. trepidation
6. jocose
7. quiescence
8. sequential
9. wainwright
10. kinetic
11. rigorous
12. yowl
13. bilingual
14. pompous
15. egalitarian
16. loquacious
17. xanthic
18. holocaust
19. unilateral
20. ambiguous
21. zenith
22. ominous
23. inept
24. deciduous
25. verification
26. gregarious

Compound Capers (page 10)

1. DOWN
2. STAND
3. FISH
4. HOUSE
5. BACK
6. HILL
7. HOP
8. KEY
9. CUP
10. WAY
11. WORK
12. BED
13. DOWN
14. PLAY
15. HAND
16. BELL
17. POST
18. GROUND
19. WALL
20. TAIL
21. OFF
22. BALL

Matching (page 70)

1. C., 2. E., 3. H., 4. E., 5. F., 6. J., 7. B., 8. A., 9. I., 10. G.

Krakatoa Map (page 94)